I0790427

WHAT?

Do You Expect From A Sinner

By Claudia Renée

Archway Publishing books may be ordered through booksellers or by contacting:

Archway Publishing
1663 Liberty Drive
Bloomington, IN 47403
www.archwaypublishing.com
844-669-3957

Scripture taken from the King James Version of the Bible.

ISBN: 978-1-6657-0865-4 (sc)
ISBN: 978-1-6657-0864-7 (hc)
ISBN: 978-1-6657-0866-1 (e)

Library of Congress Control Number: 2021912687

Print information available on the last page.

Archway Publishing rev. date: 1/24/2022

With appreciation and praise …

I praise and give thanks to my Lord and Savior, Jesus Christ. Through His Holy Spirit, He gave me this answer after I asked Him to deliver me from what I was going through in a broken relationship. My great and powerful Savior, whom I trust, love, and appreciate, has delivered me by this prophetic answer, with a question!

What?
Do You Expect From
A Sinner

With love, I dedicate this book to my Lord and Savior, Jesus Christ. For *He* has delivered me!

For all have sinned and come short of the glory of God.
—Roman 3:23 (KJV)

But the scripture hath concluded all under sin that the promise
by faith of Jesus Christ might be given to them that believe.
—Galatians 3:22 (KJV)

Amen!

In Loving Memory
of

My mother Ola Mae Young Hoye
(1927–1992)

My father William R. Hoye Sr.
(1921–1976)

My sister Ruby J. Walker
(1946–2014)

Dr. and Mrs. Myles Munroe
(1954–2014)

Sister in-Law Deborah Allen Hoye
(1952-2020)

Bishop Loran E. Mann
(1946-2021)

My sister Marsha L. Thompson
(1962-2021)

CONTENTS

PREFACE

Many people today are searching for answers to pain from relationships gone wrong, to suffering at the hands of others and problems beyond understanding.

They are searching for an answer as to why there is so much envy and hatred in the world, why there are so many killings happening and children being molested and abducted, why we can't forgive and let go, why we expect others to love and consider one another, why there is so much verbal and physical abuse, and why there is so much deception and lying taking place.

Many are being humiliated without a cause. Drug addiction is on the rise, and burglaries are unstoppable. Lusting is completely out of control. There are so many more unanswered questions.

I pray that as you read this book, you will find the answer to your questions and gain an understanding of it all.

ACKNOWLEDGMENTS

With a special thank-you
to the following people:

Cover design and layout
my daughter
Rolanda Denise Williams

Make Up By
Schatzie "Sparkle" Smith

Photographer
My nephew Chris Hoye

Assistance
My granddaughter
Bria Renée Allen

My sister
Alice Hoye Herron

Thank you, and may God continue to Bless you!

ONE

THE MISTAKEN IDENTITY

Have you ever met someone you were drawn to and befriended, and it appeared that you had a lot in common? You enjoy talking to each other, and the conversation gets longer and longer. You both are open and honest, sharing deep secrets, likes and dislikes, past and present experiences, and your joys and pains. The more you talk and laugh about things, the closer you get. You become excited and happy and start looking forward to the phone calls.

A day does not pass without a hello and wanting to hear it.

It's good when you start liking someone you're drawn to and with whom you're able to be open and honest. You can identify, gain understanding of, and have compassion for each other. I have learned that through being a good listener, I can paint a picture of what's being said. Once I become friends with someone, I consider that person as a friend. I have no reason to deceive, distrust, disbelieve, or disrespect a friend—or anyone else for that matter. It's good to treat people the way you want to be treated. I was told by someone years ago, "If you find one friend in a lifetime, you've found a friend." I couldn't believe it back then. Do you know the older I get, the more I understand?

My mother always told us, "You live and learn." I have learned that just because you can identify with a person, or you have similar life experiences or have the same likes and dislikes, it does not mean or classify him or her as a friend. This was my mistake—my big mistake!

It's so sad when you meet someone new and later find out every conversation, every kind act, every date, every message left on your voice mail, every good-morning wake-up call was motive driven. All the gifts had a reason behind them. How could I have known? What could I have thought to cause me to think that all this was a game, that what I was made to feel wasn't true or real? My mother always told me, "Everything that glitters is not gold."

I was so busy looking at the glitter that I didn't see what was behind it or what it was made of. I didn't take time to first find out the ingredients. Even dynamite glitters when it's lit. But after a while comes destruction.

Was I missing something? What did I need that I didn't know I needed? Was it something that he saw in me that he saw before in other women? Or was he a professional in the game that he was playing?

When people are good at the games they have played for so long, they know how to make the first move to start another game—and every move thereafter to the end.

Winning the game is a challenge for a sinner because he or she knows that every move is important, and losing is not an option. Once the game is over, the sinner smiles, laughs, shakes his or her head, and says, "I did it again."

Don't mistake the identity of an enemy.

Don't allow a foolish person to make a fool out of you. Don't let a sinner make a sinner out of you.

To sin is one thing, but to continue in sin is another.

Romans 3:23 (KJV) says, "For all have sinned and come short of the glory of God."

Romans 6:1–2 says, "What shall we say then? Shall we continue in sin, that grace may abound? God forbid. How shall we that are dead to sin, live any longer therein?"

So what can I do to not fall into the trap that the enemy has set for me again?

Believe me, we can't break free from sin on our own. We definitely need the Lord's help! Just trust Him!

Psalm 121:1–8 (KJV) says,

I will lift up mine eyes unto the hills from whence cometh my help.

My help cometh from the Lord which made heaven and earth.

He will not suffer thy foot to be moved: He that keepeth thee will not slumber.

Behold, he that keepeth Israel shall neither slumber nor sleep.

The Lord is thy keeper; the Lord is thy shade upon thy right hand.

The sun shall not smite thee by day, nor the moon by night.

The Lord shall preserve thee from all evil: He shall preserve thy soul.

The Lord shall preserve thy going out and thy coming in from this time forth, and even for evermore.

Amen!

The Lord will show you how to spot the player. He will teach you the moves to look out for. We all must learn from past experiences. Pay attention. Be a good listener. Don't do much talking.

The truth of the matter will always show itself. The truth of the game will surface, no matter what. No matter how interesting a person may be, don't be so easily moved or persuaded. The same way the enemy studies you, you must study the enemy.

Give it a few months, and everything you need to know about the game will be revealed—no company, no sex, no uninvited guest, and no surprise visits.

Don't be in a hurry to give out your address. And don't give out all your personal business. If you get an invitation to the movies, meet the person there. Do the same thing with a dinner date. Drive your own car. Think smart. Be smart. If you don't drive, have a friend or relative drop you off and pick you up. Watch as well as pray!

TWO
NOT SUITABLE

D o you know that we all know in the very beginning when a person is not suitable for us? How do we know? If you have a grain or mustard seed of faith in God, God will give you an unction—meaning, follow your first mind.

In 1 John 2:20 (KJV), we read, "But ye have an Unction from the Holy One and ye know all things." If you have faith and believe as you trust in God, He will warn you!"

We as human beings want and need to belong, or to have and to hold. When we get to this point in our lives, we sometimes make wrong moves, bad mistakes, wrong decisions, or bad choices, and then comes the fall.

All the signs were and will be there. If you are a Christian and meet someone who tells you he or she is not a Christian but still wants to date you—that's a sign. If the person tells you he or she believes in him- or herself—that's a sign. If you are not a Christian and you meet someone, you can tell if the person is suitable for you or not. The signs will be there.

If you meet someone and he or she tells you that you can change him or her, don't believe it. What these people are really saying is they want all your attention on them. That kind of a person will use up all your energy by having you focus on them.

If he or she disappears from Thursday to Monday every week and is not on a live-in job—that's a sign.

If the job keeps the person so busy that you can only be a ten-minute phone call a day—that's a sign.

If you get a call to see if you're going to be home this weekend and he or she doesn't show up or makes excuses—that's a sign.

When he or she calls and says he or she is on the way and then never comes over—that's a sign.

When you get let down over and over, let him or her go. Please stop and pay attention. That person is not suitable.

Amos 3:3 (KJV) says, "Can two walk together except they be agreed?"

Avoid the pain and the pitfalls of an unsuitable relationship.

Pay attention to what the person says. Listen to every word that comes out of his or her mouth. Watch for emotions and expressions. All the markings are there.

Don't miss the marks.

THREE
THE DECEPTION

You notice a change of behavior. Was it really a change of behavior, or were your eyes shut wide open because of the skills of a sinner? One of the best and highest degrees of a sinner is deception. His or her decision was already made to deceive you, for instance. When you attend a school of higher learning, you make up your mind what your profession is going to be and focus on it. So does the sinner. His or her profession is sin, so he or she focuses on sin! Everything that person needs to be good at it, he or she learns. And one of the courses of study is deception. My mother would always tell us that everything that glitters Is not Gold. Never a truer word was spoken. Everything that glitters is not God.

She would also say that the grass always looks greener on the other side. And it does! This is how we begin to be deceived. We are walking by sight.

What you can't see is the game and how it has been planned out to be played. Have you ever heard someone say, "You played me?" or "I was played?" No matter what you do, where you go, or who you meet, you always want to find out something about your object of interest. Am I right? So it is with the plan of deception. When you focus on your subject, you first must find out something about it and then study how to approach it. Then you make your move. And the game begins. Some subjects are not as easy as others. So you have to ask more questions, and more studying has to take place.

A deceiver is not looking to lose. Every move has to be the right one.

Remember that every question asked and every answer given is leading to something. Think before you answer any questions and before you give too many answers. Please do not let anyone know too much of your personal business. When the questions start coming, just say, "My life is not all that. Tell me something about you." Let him or her do the talking on the first, second, and even the third date. Even on the third date, you will find out more than what you were looking for.

One thing about a deceiver is that if he or she can't find out what he or she is looking for by the third date, you will see a flare of uneasiness. Because now you have upset his or her game plan by throwing his or her moves off. Two good things to do are be a good listener and be a good observer.

Anyone can be a deceiver—your closest friend, your neighbor, a family member, a coworker, a spouse, or even the one you're dating.

Pay attention. Watch the moves. Study the plays. Then your eyes will be open to the game. Another good piece of advice in a relationship is to listen for the same reruns, because if a deceiver was successful in a past relationship, he or she will make the same moves over and over again—because it works for him or her. Remember to keep your eyes wide open. Not wide shut!

Don't close your eyes to the facts and truth. Learn to let some things go. Learn to walk away when you see the signs and hear lies. A deceiver's lies. Deceivers lie! It is just that plain and simple.

Sin is never satisfied. Sin is a deceiver's way of life. And sin multiplies itself. Think smart, and stay five steps ahead of a sinner.

1. Don't give a sinner any more of your time once you find out his profession.
2. Disconnect the conversation—no more phone calls or texts.
3. Cut it off for good.
4. Block all numbers.
5. Erase all pictures and sweet messages.
6. Close all doors to that page in your life
7. Praise the Lord.

FOUR
OUT OF ORDER

When someone's behavior is unacceptable or wrong, that means that person is out of order.

A sinner only maintains his or her cool when necessary. Most of the time, a sinner is doing and saying wrong or unacceptable things.

If you have a bad habit of any kind, it is hard to break. How do I know? Because I had one. I was out of order at a cookout, and the Lord delivered me! The Lord has delivered me from many things!

God is able to and will deliver you from unacceptable behavior, if you ask Him!

When a sinner is out of order, these are a list of unacceptable things he or she might do:

- convey a false impression with the intent to deceive (Any untruthfulness is lying.)
- cheat at home or away
- do drugs

- fight
- kill
- steal from anyone
- stalk you
- plot against you
- start fires
- pass on diseases
- mistreat you
- say angry and offensive words
- treat you badly and want you to accept him or her as he or she is

A sinner is nasty and will want you to go along with what he or she does. A sinner has no pride or integrity. A sinner loves no one. A sinner

- is cold-hearted
- is hateful
- has no respect
- is lustful
- wears a coat of deception
- has mood swings
- stays out or away from home
- wastes money
- is unfaithful

Just to list a few!

What? Do you expect from a sinner. This is what the Lord asked me. My God, what a question! And what an answer! I was instantly delivered!

Why do we expect a sinner to do the right things when righteousness is not in him or her? He is out of order! Completely out of order!

FIVE

THE POWER OF THE SIN STRICKEN

Now your eyes are open to being wounded, in pain, hurt, and broken-hearted and to suffering. The sad thing about being stricken with the pain of love is deception and untruth. And it shows up unexpectedly. Your emotions take a drastic turn that you didn't know existed. You discover something about yourself that you don't like. Your ways begin to change. Rage and anger take hold of you. Things that you never thought about begin to enter your mind. Things you never did before, you start doing. You are acting totally out of character.

This is not you.

Being stricken by the power of sin brings on unusual behavior. You are out of control of yourself, and you start doing things you never did before. You are losing sleep, can't eat, and are making dumb mistakes.

The power of someone who is a sinner now has an effect on you. You've been stricken. When a sinner strikes one time, rest assured, he or she will strike again.

You can believe he or she has done this to someone else before. Why do we expect a sinner to do the right thing?

A sinner has an occupation, and that occupation is sin. That's his or her professional vocation. A sinner is good at what he or she does. The sinner studies to do what he or she does and practices on you. He or she gains experience, learns how to perfect his or her skills, and becomes a professional. A sinner occupies his or her office to take possession of whatever or whomever he or she can. To have and to hold!

A sinner will have your mind and hold on to your heart if you let him or her. And if you let him or her, the sinner will take up residence. Do you want to know what is so sad?

The next one, you may know. It could be a best friend, a neighbor, a business partner, a family member, or a coworker. You can't hate the next one because he or she has been stricken also, just like you were.

The grass always looks greener on the other side of the fence, and it doesn't matter who is spraying the lawn.

Think about all the fish in the sea. No matter how long they have been swimming together, it's all about the bait. First come, first served. All the others fall in line to be next. If he or she treats you well, you both will make it known. You will tell it, and he or she will show it. It's all a part of the game plan.

The next one is easy picking from there on in. All fish rush to the bait. It's easy catching now!

Pay attention. Don't be played, don't be used, don't be duped, and don't be a trick.

Yes, the sinner will dress you, feed you, flaunt you because he or she has to show you off. This is how he or she is preparing for the next victim! When the sinner ditches you, he or she has found his or her next catch. Think it not strange. This is the work and way of a sinner. He or she will cause you to be deceived and stricken.

In order to be taken in and captured by a sinner, you first have to be attracted to the bait. And so on the forbidden road you go!

A sinner will take you where you don't want to go and keep you longer than you want to stay!

SIX

SIN OR SICKNESS

L et's look at sin again. It means an immoral act, considered to be a transgression against the divine law of Almighty God. Sinful acts or deeds are choices made with your own free will of action. Sin is a negative force in the human existence, compelling us to do ungodly things, such as wicked, deliberate, unremorseful, hateful, plotted, and criminal acts—all of this and then some. When done over and over again, these habitual acts are what makes a sinner.

Greed, lust, envy, gluttony, anger, rage, bitterness, and unforgiveness can encourage and bring on sin.

Once sin has taken hold of you, the things that encouraged you to sin will be the same things to nurture the sin in you.

Sin is a decision or choice.

James 4:17 (KJV) says, "Therefore to Him that knoweth to do good, and doeth it not, to Him it is sin."

I believe that all sinners have at one point or another evaluated their course of action before committing sin and decided to move forward to do it. From there, they decided to continue in it over and over. Now, they are insensitive, having or showing no concern for others' feelings and having abandoned righteousness altogether.

Sin has mastered your behavior and has taken total control of you.

Sin is a strong force of the devil, and only God Almighty Himself can deliver you from it.

Now, let's look at sickness. Sickness is having ill health and disorder, being in a weakened or unsound condition. Sickness is an unhealthy condition of the body or mind, the state of being sick. It can be a specific type of disease, such as sleeping sickness or motion sickness. Any type of illness that one may have should be seen and treated by a medical doctor for healing.

Sin cannot be, nor should it be, linked with sickness.

Go to a medical doctor for sickness.

Go to God for sin!

SEVEN
IT WASN'T MEANT FOR YOU

Have you ever been introduced to someone by a friend who wanted to matchmake or pair you up with someone? Your friends, knowing the kind of person you are drawn to, said they found the right one for you. Some things matter to certain people when meeting someone new but do not matter to others.

It could be the smile, the eyes, the height, the conversation, the complexion, the looks, the feet, or anything that excites or turns you on. I have learned to look a little deeper than what meets the eye. All the makings of a sinner do not meet the eyes. Some are always hidden at first glance.

What a person looks like does not mean a hill of beans. Looks don't make a man or woman. It's all about what's on the inside. Some of the best-looking, best-dressed, best conversationalists are the worst mates. They focus on themselves only. You are out of the picture because it's all about them.

Take a mental note. Looks are deceiving, and so is a sinner.

The real face and features are not what you see or what you are looking for. The mask is on, and so is the performance. Now the show begins.

Would you believe the first sign of abuse can be seen on the first date if you knew he or she was an abuser?

The same goes for a cheater or a liar.

You can spot an abuser on the first date by how he or she speaks. An abuser will speak with a voice of courtesy or in a controlling tone. If it is controlling on the first or second date, this person is not meant for you! Back up, back out, and stay out. Because it's just the beginning.

Do not let anyone control or dominate you. Don't be a target for an abusive sinner. He or she will try to make you feel unworthy and worthless. These people will put you down if you or things don't go their way.

Abusive sinners want you to cater to them and them only. They want you to submit to their demands. You become manipulated by their ultimatums.

This person is not for you. Do not expect good to come out of it! The Lord will protect you from what is not meant for you. Obey!

EIGHT
THE WRONG SIDE

A sinner occupies his or her time and energy with the one most important thing to him or her, which is sin. It's so hard to believe that no matter what good he or she does, sin is in the front of it. This is so sad. This kind of person will go all out to do you in. They will even get a job at your place of employment just to watch you. They want to compete and to know how you are doing on the job just to hurt you. Satan has a field day and night with sinners.

These kinds of people live on the wrong side of life, of heaven, and of God.

The door of repentance is open if they choose to enter in, if they choose to turn away from sin and live in the abundant life, which is free and has been paid for by our Lord and Savior, Jesus Christ, for all.

I tried *Jesus*, I turned, I repented, and praise the Lord, I am no longer on the wrong side!

Thank You, Jesus.

Acts 2:1–47 says,

Pentecost: first baptism of men with the Holy Spirit
(note a, Mt. 3:6; Jn. 7:37)

AND when the day of Pĕn'tecŏst was fully come, they were all with one accord in one place.

2 And suddenly there came a sound from heaven as of a rushing mighty wind, and it filled all the house where they were sitting.

3 And there appeared unto them cloven tongues like as of fire, and it sat upon each of them.

4 And they were all filled with the Hō'lў Ghöst, and began to speak with other tongues, as the Spirit gave them utterance.

Effect of the Holy Spirit baptism on the people

5 And there were dwelling at Jerusalem Jews, devout men, out of every nation under heaven.

6 Now when this was noised abroad, the multitude came together, and were confounded, because that every man heard them speak in his own language.

7 And they were all amazed and marvelled, saying one to another, Behold, are not all these which speak Găl-ĭlæ'ans?

8 And how hear we every man in our own tongue, wherein we were born?

9 Pär'thĭans, and Mēdes, and Ē'lam-ïtes, and the dwellers in Mĕs-o-potā'mĭà, and in Jūdæ'ä, and Căp-pa-dō'çí-à, Pŏn'tus, and in, Ā'ṣià,

10 Phrўğ'ĭ-à, and Păm-phў'l'ĭ-à, in Ēġў'pt, and in the parts of Lĭb'ў̆-à about Çȳ-rēn and strangers of Röme, Jews and proselytes,

11 Crētes and Ā-rā'bĭ-an<u>s</u>, we do hear them speak in our tongues the wonderful works of God.

12 And they were all amazed, and were in doubt, saying one to another, What meaneth this?

13 Others mocking said, These men are full of new wine.

III Revival at Jerusalem (Acts 2:14–8:3. Cp. 8:4; 11:19) 1 First apostolic sermon:
(1) Preacher and his audience

14 But Pē'tēr, standing up with the eleven, lifted up his voice, and said unto them, Ye men of Jū-dæ'à, and all *ye* that dwell at Jerusalĕm, be this known unto you, and hearken to my words:

(2) Joel's prophecy fulfilled (Joel 2:28)

15 For these are not drunken, as ye suppose, seeing it is *but* the third hour of the day.

★16 But this is that which was spoken by the prophet Jō'el;

(3) Prediction of Joel's prophecy being fulfilled again in the "last days"

★17 And it shall come to pass in the last days, saith God, I will pour out of my Spirit upon all flesh: and your sons and your daughters shall prophesy, and your young men shall see visions, and your old men shall dream dreams:

18 And on my servants and on my handmaidens I will pour out in those days of my Spirit; and they shall prophesy:

(4) Even in the future tribulation men will be saved and baptized in the Holy Spirit (Joel 2:28; Zech. 12:10–13:7; Rev. 6:9–11; 7:14)

19 And I will shew wonders in heaven above, and signs in the earth beneath: blood, and fire, and vapour of smoke:

20 The sun shall be turned into darkness, and the moon into blood, before that great and notable day of the Lord come:

21 And it shall come to pass, *that* whosoever shall call on the name of the Lord shall be saved.

(5) Jesus approved of God

22 Ye men of Is′ra-el, hear these words; Jē′sus of Năz′arĕth, a man approved of God among you by miracles and wonders and signs, which God did by him in the midst of you, as ye yourselves also know:

(6) The crucifixion of Jesus fulfilled God's plan (Gen. 3: 15; Isa. 53; Ps. 22)

23 Him, being delivered by the determinate counsel and foreknowledge of God, ye have taken, and by wicked hands have crucified and slain:

(7) The resurrection of Jesus fulfilled prophecy (Ps. 16:9–10; 110:1, 5)

24 Whom God hath raised up, having loosed the pains of death: because it was not possible that he should be holden of it.

25 For Dā'vid speaketh concerning him, I foresaw the Lord always before my face, for he is on my right hand, that I should not be moved:

26 Therefore did my heart rejoice, and my tongue was glad; moreover also my flesh shall rest in hope:

27 Because thou wilt not leave my soul in hell, neither wilt thou suffer thine Holy One to see corruption.

28 Thou hast made known to me the ways of life; thou shalt make me full of joy with thy countenance.

29. Men *and* brethren, let me freely speak unto you of the patriarch Dā'vid, that he is both dead and buried, and his sepulchre is with us unto this day.

★30 Therefore being a prophet, and knowing that God had sworn with an oath to him, that of the fruit of his loins, according to the flesh, he would raise up Christ to sit on his throne;

★31 He seeing this before spake of the resurrection of Christ, that his soul was not left in hell, neither his flesh did see corruption.

32 This Jē'ṣus hath God raised up, whereof we all are witnesses.

(8) Jesus has ascended to heaven and the Spirit baptism you SEE and HEAR is proof of it (Jn. 7:39; 14:16–26; 15:26; 16:7–15)

33 Therefore being by the right hand of God exalted, and having received of the Father the promise of the Hō'lyˇ Ghōst, he hath shed forth this, which ye now see and hear.

★34 For Dā'vid is not ascended into the heavens: but he saith himself. "The LORD said unto my Lord, Sit thou on my right hand,
35 Until I make thy foes thy footstool.

(9) God has made Jesus both LORD and CHRIST (Acts 2:26)

36 Therefore let all the house of Ĭs'ra-el know assuredly, that God hath made that same Jē'sus, whom ye have crucified, both Lord and Christ.

2 Effect of Peter's sermon (v 41; 4:4; 5:33)

37 Now when they heard *this*, they were pricked in their heart, and said unto Pē'tēr and to the rest of the apostles, Men *and* brethren, what shall we do?

3 What all sinners must do (Lk. 13:1–5; 24:47; 1 Jn. 1:9)

38 Then Pē'tēr said unto them, Repent, and be baptized every one of you in the name of Jē's̲us Chrīst for the remission of sins, and ye shall receive the gift of the Hō'ly̆ Ghöst.

4 Spirit baptism promised to all believers (Mt. 3:11; Lk. 11:14; Jn. 7:37–39; Gal. 3:14)

39 For the promise is unto you, and to your children, and to all that are afar off, *even* as many as the Lord our God shall call.

5 Many unwritten exhortations (Cp. Jn. 21:25)

40 And with many other words did he testify and exhort, saying, Save yourselves from this untoward generation.

3,000 converted (Cp. 4:4)

41 Then they that gladly received his word were baptized: and the same day there were added *unto them* about three thousand souls.

Glorious state of the early church (4:32; 5:12; 6:1)

42 And they continued stedfastly in the apostles' doctrine and fellowship, and in breaking of bread, and in prayers.
43 And fear came upon every soul: and many wonders and signs were done by the apostles.
44 And all that believed were together, and had all things common;
45 And sold their possessions and goods, and parted them to all *men*, as every man had need.
46 And they, continuing daily with one accord in the temple, and breaking bread from house to house, did eat their meat with gladness and singleness of heart,
47 Praising God, and having favour with all the people. And the Lord added to the church daily such as should be saved.

NINE
THE WICKED AND UNJUST ACT

L et us look at the wicked and unjust sinner. To be labeled or put in a class of wickedness, one must be capable of harming someone or something, be cruel, and act in an evil way.

Wicked people do not stop. They cannot stop. They don't think, and they don't listen. There is no rule of righteousness in the mind of the wicked.

The state of mind in a wicked person is evil. The act of wickedness does not conform to what is right. These people live in a thick fog of darkness and can't break free from it, because they have been overtaken by a wicked spirit.

I am a firm believer that prayer changes things.

In 2 Chronicles 7:14 (KJV), we read, "If my people who are called by my name will humble themselves and pray and seek my face, and turn from their wicked ways, then I will hear from heaven, and will forgive their sin and heal their land."

Numbers 23:19 (KJV) says, "God is not a man that He should lie.

Nor a son of man that He should repent! Has He said and will He not do? Or has He spoken, and will He not make it good!"

Our God knows how to deliver us. Just believe and put your trust in Him. He is so wise, so mighty, so powerful, and such an awesome friend. There is nothing He can't do!

I know what my God can do. I have called on Him more than once, and He heard my call, my cry, my prayer, and *He*, yes, every time came and delivered me!

He has all power over the wicked spirits, over evil, over injustice, and over the hateful acts of the wicked.

There is hope for the worst of us, hope for the least of us. There is hope for the best of us, and there is hope for those who think more highly of themselves than they ought to. There is hope for all!

PSALM 44

Fifth Psalm of Instruction (on help in distress)
To the chief Musician for the sons of Korah, Maschil (instruction). 1
Eightfold deliverance by God of Israel under Joshua

WE have heard with our ears, O God, our fathers have told us, *what* work thou didst in their days, in the times of old.
2 *How* thou didst drive out the heathen with thy hand, and plantedst them; *how* thou didst afflict the people, and cast them out.
3 For they got not the land in possession by their own sword, neither did their own arm save them: but thy right hand, and thine arm, and the light of thy countenance, because thou hadst a favour unto them.

Eightfold confidence in God as Israel's Deliverer

4 Thou art my King, O God: command deliverances for Jā'cob.
5 Through thee will we push down our enemies: through thy name will we tread them under that rise up against us.
6 For I will not trust in my bow, neither shall my sword save me.
7 But thou hast saved us from our enemies, and hast put them to shame that hated us.
8 In God we boast all the day long, and praise thy name for ever. Sē'lah.

Sixteenfold judgment on Israel: God blamed for sufferings

9 But thou hast cast off, and put us to shame; and goest not forth with
our armies.

10 Thou makest us to turn back from the enemy: and they which hate
us spoil for themselves.

11 Thou hast given us like sheep *appointed* for meat; and hast scattered
us among the heathen.

12 Thou sellest thy people for nought, and dost not increase *thy wealth*
by their price.

13 Thou makest us a reproach to our neighbours, a scorn and a derision
to them that are round about us.

14 Thou makest us a byword among the heathen, a shaking of the head
among the people.

15 My confusion *is* continually before me, and the shame of my face
hath covered me,

16 For the voice of him that reproacheth and blasphemeth; by reason
of the enemy and avenger.

Eightfold accusation of God and declaration of innocence

17 All this is come upon us; yet have we not forgotten thee, neither have
we dealt falsely in thy covenant.

18 Our heart is not turned back, neither have our steps declined from
thy way;

19 Though thou hast sore broken us in the place of dragons, and covered
us with the shadow of death.

20 If we have forgotten the name of our God, or stretched out our hands
to a strange god;

21 Shall not God search this out? for he knoweth the secrets of the
heart.

22 Yea, for thy sake are we killed all the day long; we are counted as
sheep for the slaughter.

Eightfold prayer for deliverance from distress

23 Awake, why sleepest thou, O Lord? arise, cast *us* not off for ever.

24 Wherefore hidest thou thy face, *and* forgettest our affliction and
    our oppression?

25 For our soul is bowed down to the dust: our belly cleaveth unto the
    earth.

26 Arise for our help, and redeem us for thy mercies' sake.

PSALM 43

Eleventh Prayer of Distress

Eightfold request for deliverance from distress

JUDGE me, O God, and plead my cause against an ungodly nation: O
    deliver me from the deceitful and unjust man.
2 For thou *art* the God of my strength: why dost thou cast me off? Why
    go I mourning because of the oppression of the enemy?
3 O send out thy light and thy truth: let them lead me; let them bring
    me unto thy holy hill, and to thy tabernacles.

THEN: 3 promises to God

4 Then will I go unto the altar of God, unto God my exceeding joy: yea,
    upon the harp will I praise thee, O God my God.

Fourfold appeal to the soul (42:5, 11)

5 Why art thou cast down, O my soul? and why art thou disquieted
    within me? hope in God: for I shall yet praise him, *who is* the
    health of my countenance, and my God.

TEN

KNOW RIGHT FROM WRONG

Let us ask ourselves, *Do we take time to ask this question: "Is it right or wrong?" before we do something?* For instance, I am trying to lose weight, and I see ice cream on sale three for ten dollars, so I ask myself, Do I buy three or just one? Should I pass on all three? I decided to get all three and eat a little at a time. I didn't eat just a little because a little was not satisfying. So I added on more weight. A lot of our problems, mistakes, bad choices, and wrong moves are our own fault.

Many uncomfortable relationships can be avoided if we ask ourselves, "Is it right or wrong?"

If you have an uncertainty about something or someone, don't do it! As I stated before, the Lord will give you an unction. Obey!

If there is any possibility that makes you say, "No, this is not right," then back away from it, because it is wrong.

Don't force right into something that is wrong. My mother always told us, "Right is right, and wrong is wrong, and right don't wrong no one!"

If we consent to do wrong, take part in sin, we reap what we sow. That's a fact.

Galatians 6:7 (KJV) says, "Be not deceived; God is not mocked: for whatsoever a man soweth, that shall he also reap."

Yes! I have reaped the wrong that I've done, and it's not good by any means. I praise the Lord it's in my past. Reaping is so much more painful than the wrong. It hurts!

My mother also said, "Tell the truth, and shame the devil!"

I am so happy. I've been delivered and set free from wrong. Praise the Lord! Jesus is a friend of mine.

John 8:36 (KJV) says, "If the son therefore shall make you free, ye shall be free indeed."

ELEVEN

WHAT ONE THINKS IS GOOD TURNS OUT TO BE BAD

This is one of my favorite stories in the Bible; it shows just how merciful and forgiving our Lord is.

Acts 22:1–30 (KJV) says,

Men, brethren, and fathers, hear ye my defence which I make now unto you.

2 (And when they heard that he spake in the Hebrew tongue to them, they kept the more silence: and he saith,)

3 I am verily a man which am a Jew, born in Tarsus, a city in Cilicia, yet brought up in this city at the feet of Gamaliel, and taught according to the perfect manner of the law of the fathers, and was zealous toward God, as ye all are this day.

4 And I persecuted this way unto the death, binding and delivering into prisons both men and women.

5 As also the high priest doth bear me witness, and all the estate of the elders: from whom also I received letters unto the brethren, and went to Damascus, to bring them which were there bound unto Jerusalem, for to be punished.

6 And it came to pass, that, as I made my journey, and was come nigh unto Damascus about noon, suddenly there shone from heaven a great light round about me.

7 And I fell unto the ground, and heard a voice saying unto me, Saul, Saul, why persecutest thou me?

8 And I answered, Who art thou, Lord? And he said unto me, I am Jesus of Nazareth, whom thou persecutest.

9 And they that were with me saw indeed the light, and were afraid; but they heard not the voice of him that spake to me.

10 And I said, What shall I do, Lord? And the Lord said unto me, Arise, and go into Damascus; and there it shall be told thee of all things which are appointed for thee to do.

11 And when I could not see for the glory of that light, being led by the hand of them that were with me, I came into Damascus.

12 And one Ananias, a devout man according to the law, having a good report of all the Jews which dwelt there,

13 Came unto me, and stood, and said unto me, Brother Saul, receive thy sight. And the same hour I looked up upon him.

14 And he said, The God of our fathers hath chosen thee, that thou shouldest know his will, and see that Just One, and shouldest hear the voice of his mouth.

15 For thou shalt be his witness unto all men of what thou hast seen and heard.

16 And now why tarriest thou? arise, and be baptized, and wash away thy sins, calling on the name of the Lord.

17 And it came to pass, that, when I was come again to Jerusalem, even while I prayed in the temple, I was in a trance;

18 And saw him saying unto me, Make haste, and get thee quickly out of Jerusalem: for they will not receive thy testimony concerning me.

19 And I said, Lord, they know that I imprisoned and beat in every synagogue them that believed on thee:

20 And when the blood of thy martyr Stephen was shed, I also was standing by, and consenting unto his death, and kept the raiment of them that slew him.

21 And he said unto me, Depart: for I will send thee far hence unto the Gĕn'tīleṣ.

Paul rescued from the mob

22 And they gave him audience unto this word, and *then* lifted up their voices, and said, Away with such a *fellow* from the earth: for it is not fit that he should live.

23 And as they cried out, and cast off *their* clothes, and threw dust into the air,

24 The chief captain commanded him to be brought into the castle, and bade that he should be examined

by scourging; that he might know wherefore they cried so against him.

Paul a Roman citizen

25 And as they bound him with thongs, Paul said unto the centurion that stood by, Is it lawful for you to scourge a man that is a Rō'man, and uncondemned? 26 When the centurion heard *that*, he went and told the chief captain, saying, Take heed what thou doest: for this man is a Rō'man.
27 Then the chief captain came, and said unto him, Tell me, art thou a Rō'man? He said, Yea.
28 And the chief captain answered, With a great sum obtained I this freedom. And Paul said, But I was *free* born.
29 Then straightway they departed from him which should have examined him: and the chief captain also was afraid, after he knew that he was a Rō'man, and because he had bound him.
30 On the morrow, because he would have known the certainty wherefore he was accused of the Jews, he loosed him from *his* bands, and commanded the chief priests and all their council to appear and brought Paul down, and set him before them.

So Saul, whose name was changed to Paul, gave his testimony of one who thought what was good was all bad. His thoughts and acts were all wrong.

TWELVE
THE TURN AROUND

After the no-shows and lies that I was getting from him, I decided to see if what I thought was true actually was. He told me he was going to be out of town for the weekend, and I didn't believe him. He said that he was leaving Friday morning and would not be back until Monday evening. Knowing the kind of work he did, I thought it was possible. But I had an unction that was telling me it was not so.

So at midnight—yes, *midnight*—I decided to drive thirty minutes from my house to chase a lie. Now, was it worth all that? I was losing sleep, in my car driving late at night, and anger set in because of my emotions. Everything ungodly was going through my mind—all the what-ifs and then all the questions: why? Then hurt stepped on board. I was at this point, a complete mess.

God is so awesomely amazing. Here I am at a red light, at midnight! Red light means stop! No go! Wait! Be still! Don't move or proceed forward! This was an answer in itself. But it wasn't enough for me.

I needed God to do something. I needed *Him* to fix me because

I was broken, and I needed to be mended. My mind was in turmoil. I needed God's help.

I stopped at the red light and made my request known unto God. I asked Him to deliver me, and I meant it! I was acting completely out of character.

My great God heard me, helped me, and delivered me!

He said to me, "What? What do you expect from a sinner?"

Instantly, the Lord did it. My mind was restored and renewed. He gave me something new to think about.

I did a U-turn. I turned around, went back home, went to bed, and went to sleep!

What? Do you expect from a sinner

Delivered?

THIRTEEN

THE CONCLUSION OF THE MATTER

After you have read this book in its entirety, I pray that you will be able to forgive, let go, and be healed of all past hurts and failures.

I pray that now you will know and recognize what and who you were dealing with. You, like I did, expected a lot more from someone who failed you.

Now, you know that he or she did what he or she knew to do and what was in him or her to do, which was sin.

As humans, we look for more out of others than what is in them. They don't have in them what we expect. They don't know, and we take too much for granted, thinking that they do know.

Sinners find leisure in what they do, so they continue to sin over and over again.

Proverbs 16:27 (KJV) says, "An ungodly man diggeth up evil; and in his lips there is as a burning fire."

Don't expect a sinner to do the right thing or to live a righteous life, when he or she is ungodly.

Proverbs 16:22 (KJV) says, "Understanding is a well spring of life unto him that hath it but the instruction of fools is folly."

Don't be enticed by a sinner.

Don't give up your right way and do wrong.

Don't be a partaker of sin.

Don't be lured or tempted.

Don't be manipulated.

PROVERBS 4:1–27

YE CHILDREN: fourteen commands: fourteen blessings

HEAR, ye children, the instruction of a father, and attend to know
  understanding.
2 For I give you good doctrine, forsake ye not my law.
3 For I was my father's son, tender and only *beloved* in the sight of my
  mother.
4 He taught me also, and said unto me, Let thine heart retain my words:
  keep my commandments, and live.
5 Get wisdom, get understanding: forget *it* not; neither decline from
  the words of my mouth.
6 Forsake her not, and she shall preserve thee: love her and she shall
  keep thee.
7 Wisdom *is* the principal thing; *therefore* get wisdom: and with all thy
  getting get understanding.
8 Exalt her, and she shall promote thee: she shall bring thee to honour,
  when thou dost embrace her.
9 She shall give to thine head an ornament of grace: a crown of glory
  shall she deliver to thee.

MY SON: (1) Two commands: five blessings

10 Hear, O my son, and receive my savings; and the years of thy life
  shall be many.

11 I have taught thee in the way of wisdom; I have led thee in right
paths.

12 When thou goest, thy steps shall not be straitened; and when thou
runnest, thou shalt not stumble.

Nine commands: nine blessings

13 Take fast hold of instruction; let *her* not go: keep her; for she *is* thy
life.

14 Enter not into the path of the wicked, and go not in the way of evil
men.

15 Avoid it, pass not by it, turn from it, and pass away.

16 For they sleep not, except they have done mischief; and their sleep
is taken away, unless they cause *some* to fall.

17 For they eat the bread of wickedness, and drink the wine of violence.

18 But the path of the just *is* as the shining light, that shineth more and
more unto the perfect day.

19 The way of the wicked *is* as darkness: they know not at what they
stumble.

MY SON: (1) Four commands: four blessings

20 My son, attend to my words; incline thine ear unto my sayings.

21 Let them not depart from thine eyes; keep them in the midst of
thine heart.

22 For they *are* life unto those that find them, and health to all their
flesh.

Ten commands: ten blessings

23 Keep thy heart with all diligence; for out of it *are* the issues of life.

24. Put away from thee a froward mouth, and perverse lips put far from
thee.

25 Let thine eyes look right on, and let thine eyelids look straight before
   thee.
26 Ponder the path of thy feet, and let all thy ways be established.
27 Turn not to the right hand nor to the left: remove thy foot from evil.

If you let a sinner take you where you don't want to go, he or she will keep you longer than you want to stay. And breaking free will take God's help.

Proverbs 16:20 says, "He that handleth a matter wisely shall find good: and whoso trusteth in the LORD, happy is he."

So we ask God, "Why did this happen?"

"Why does it hurt so bad? How can I make it?"

"When will it pass?"

"How long do I have to suffer?"

"Why can't I stop crying?"

"Why was I mistreated?

"Why didn't he love me?"

"What did I do wrong?"

"Why did it happen like this?"

There are so many questions.

My one request to God was, "Lord, deliver me from this."

I was at a red light at midnight, going thirty minutes out of my way to chase a lie.

God in His mighty awesome power and wisdom gave me this profound, prophetic answer with this question:

What?
Do You Expect From A Sinner

I was instantly delivered, healed, and set free by God Almighty. As I said, I did a U-turn, went home and went to sleep.

Fivefold prayer for blessing

15 Wherefore I also, after I heard of your faith in the Lord Jē′ṣus, and
　　love unto all the saints,

16 Cease not to give thanks for you, making mention of you in my
　　prayers;

17 That the God of our Lord Jē′ṣus Chrīst, the Father of glory, may give
　　unto you the spirit of wisdom and revelation in the knowledge of
　　him:

18 The eyes of your understanding being enlightened; that ye may
　　know what is the hope of his calling, and what the riches of the
　　glory of his inheritance in the saints,

19 And what *is* the exceeding greatness of his power to us-ward who
　　believe, according to the working of his mighty power,

3 Tenfold greatness of power (Mt. 28:18; Jn. 14:12–15; 1 Pet. 3:22)

20 Which he wrought in Christ, when he raised him from the dead, and
　　set *him* at his own right hand in the heavenly *places,*

21 Far above all principality, and power, and might, and dominion, and
　　every name that is named, not only in this world, but also in that
　　which is to come:

22 And hath put all *things* under his feet, and gave him *to be* the head
　　over all *things* to the church.

23 Which is his body, the fullness of him that filleth all in all.

Let's take a look at just what sin is, or rather the definition of sin. It means the breaking of a religious law—to do wrong, especially when it has been planned, plotted, and purposed. Sin is a wrongdoing, an unjust act. It is a purposeful pain given or done to someone or something. It is to commit a crime, a wrong, or a fault, to do wrong and not right. It is bad, not good. Unlawful and wicked sin makes a sinner. So goes the sinner who now is dishonest and lives in error. The sinner has no compassion; is cold-hearted, hateful, unremorseful, deceiving, distrusting, sneaky, cunning, a liar, and hateful; and cares about no one and nothing. A sinner lives in a mind and place of unrest. They live a life of always having to look over their shoulders, and feels uncomfortable no matter where they are.

Yet a sinner calls him- or herself good at what he or she does. A sinner is never satisfied, until he or she receives a degree in sin and is labeled a professional!

What?
Do You Expect From A Sinner

Remember this!

A sinner will take you where you don't want to go and keep you longer than you want to stay!

—Claudia Renée

THE BOOK OF PROVERBS

The proverbs of Solomon the son of David, king of Israel;

2 To know wisdom and instruction; to perceive the words of understanding;

3 To receive the instruction of wisdom, justice, and judgment, and equity;

4 To give subtilty to the simple, to the young man knowledge and discretion.

5 A wise man will hear, and will increase learning; and a man of understanding shall attain unto wise counsels:

6 To understand a proverb, and the interpretation; the words of the wise, and their dark sayings.

7 The fear of the Lord is the beginning of knowledge: but fools despise wisdom and instruction.

8 My son, hear the instruction of thy father, and forsake not the law of thy mother:

9 For they shall be an ornament of grace unto thy head, and chains about thy neck.

10 My son, if sinners entice thee, consent thou not.

11 If they say, Come with us, let us lay wait for blood, let us lurk privily for the innocent without cause:

12 Let us swallow them up alive as the grave; and whole, as those that go down into the pit:

13 We shall find all precious substance, we shall fill our houses with spoil:

14 Cast in thy lot among us; let us all have one purse:

15 My son, walk not thou in the way with them; refrain thy foot from their path:

16 For their feet run to evil, and make haste to shed blood.

17 Surely in vain the net is spread in the sight of any bird.

18 And they lay wait for their own blood; they lurk privily for their own lives.

19 So are the ways of every one that is greedy of gain; which taketh away the life of the owners thereof.

20 Wisdom crieth without; she uttereth her voice in the streets:

21 She crieth in the chief place of concourse, in the openings of the gates: in the city she uttereth her words, saying,

22 How long, ye simple ones, will ye love simplicity? and the scorners delight in their scorning, and fools hate knowledge?

23 Turn you at my reproof: behold, I will pour out my spirit unto you, I will make known my words unto you.

24 Because I have called, and ye refused; I have stretched out my hand, and no man regarded;

25 But ye have set at nought all my counsel, and would none of my reproof:

26 I also will laugh at your calamity; I will mock when your fear cometh;

27 When your fear cometh as desolation, and your destruction cometh as a whirlwind; when distress and anguish cometh upon you.

28 Then shall they call upon me, but I will not answer; they shall seek me early, but they shall not find me:

29 For that they hated knowledge, and did not choose the fear of the Lord:

30 They would none of my counsel: they despised all my reproof.

31 Therefore shall they eat of the fruit of their own way, and be filled with their own devices.

32 For the turning away of the simple shall slay them, and the prosperity of fools shall destroy them.

33 But whoso hearkeneth unto me shall dwell safely, and shall be quiet from fear of evil.

Proverbs Chapter 2

My son, if thou wilt receive my words, and hide my commandments with thee;

2 So that thou incline thine ear unto wisdom, and apply thine heart to understanding;

3 Yea, if thou criest after knowledge, and liftest up thy voice for understanding;

4 If thou seekest her as silver, and searchest for her as for hid treasures;

5 Then shalt thou understand the fear of the Lord, and find the knowledge of God.

6 For the Lord giveth wisdom: out of his mouth cometh knowledge and understanding.

7 He layeth up sound wisdom for the righteous: he is a buckler to them that walk uprightly.

8 He keepeth the paths of judgment, and preserveth the way of his saints.

9 Then shalt thou understand righteousness, and judgment, and equity; yea, every good path.

10 When wisdom entereth into thine heart, and knowledge is pleasant unto thy soul;

11 Discretion shall preserve thee, understanding shall keep thee:

12 To deliver thee from the way of the evil man, from the man that speaketh froward things;

13 Who leave the paths of uprightness, to walk in the ways of darkness;

14 Who rejoice to do evil, and delight in the frowardness of the wicked;

15 Whose ways are crooked, and they froward in their paths:

16 To deliver thee from the strange woman, even from the stranger which flattereth with her words;

17 Which forsaketh the guide of her youth, and forgetteth the covenant of her God.

18 For her house inclineth unto death, and her paths unto the dead.

19 None that go unto her return again, neither take they hold of the paths of life.

20 That thou mayest walk in the way of good men, and keep the paths of the righteous.

21 For the upright shall dwell in the land, and the perfect shall remain in it.

22 But the wicked shall be cut off from the earth, and the transgressors shall be rooted out of it.

Proverbs Chapter 3

My son, forget not my law; but let thine heart keep my commandments:

2 For length of days, and long life, and peace, shall they add to thee.

3 Let not mercy and truth forsake thee: bind them about thy neck; write them upon the table of thine heart:

4 So shalt thou find favour and good understanding in the sight of God and man.

5 Trust in the Lord with all thine heart; and lean not unto thine own understanding.

6 In all thy ways acknowledge him, and he shall direct thy paths.

7 Be not wise in thine own eyes: fear the Lord, and depart from evil.

8 It shall be health to thy navel, and marrow to thy bones.

9 Honour the Lord with thy substance, and with the firstfruits of all thine increase:

10 So shall thy barns be filled with plenty, and thy presses shall burst out with new wine.

11 My son, despise not the chastening of the Lord; neither be weary of his correction:

12 For whom the Lord loveth he correcteth; even as a father the son in whom he delighteth.

13 Happy is the man that findeth wisdom, and the man that getteth understanding.

14 For the merchandise of it is better than the merchandise of silver, and the gain thereof than fine gold.

15 She is more precious than rubies: and all the things thou canst desire are not to be compared unto her.

16 Length of days is in her right hand; and in her left hand riches and honour.

17 Her ways are ways of pleasantness, and all her paths are peace.

18 She is a tree of life to them that lay hold upon her: and happy is every one that retaineth her.

19 The Lord by wisdom hath founded the earth; by understanding hath he established the heavens.

20 By his knowledge the depths are broken up, and the clouds drop down the dew.

21 My son, let not them depart from thine eyes: keep sound wisdom and discretion:

22 So shall they be life unto thy soul, and grace to thy neck.

23 Then shalt thou walk in thy way safely, and thy foot shall not stumble.

24 When thou liest down, thou shalt not be afraid: yea, thou shalt lie down, and thy sleep shall be sweet.

25 Be not afraid of sudden fear, neither of the desolation of the wicked, when it cometh.

26 For the Lord shall be thy confidence, and shall keep thy foot from being taken.

27 Withhold not good from them to whom it is due, when it is in the power of thine hand to do it.

28 Say not unto thy neighbour, Go, and come again, and to morrow I will give; when thou hast it by thee.

29 Devise not evil against thy neighbour, seeing he dwelleth securely by thee.

30 Strive not with a man without cause, if he have done thee no harm.

31 Envy thou not the oppressor, and choose none of his ways.

32 For the froward is abomination to the Lord: but his secret is with the righteous.

33 The curse of the Lord is in the house of the wicked: but he blesseth the habitation of the just.

34 Surely he scorneth the scorners: but he giveth grace unto the lowly.

35 The wise shall inherit glory: but shame shall be the promotion of fools.

Proverbs Chapter 4

Hear, ye children, the instruction of a father, and attend to know understanding.

2 For I give you good doctrine, forsake ye not my law.

3 For I was my father's son, tender and only beloved in the sight of my mother.

4 He taught me also, and said unto me, Let thine heart retain my words: keep my commandments, and live.

5 Get wisdom, get understanding: forget it not; neither decline from the words of my mouth.

6 Forsake her not, and she shall preserve thee: love her, and she shall keep thee.

7 Wisdom is the principal thing; therefore get wisdom: and with all thy getting get understanding.

8 Exalt her, and she shall promote thee: she shall bring thee to honour, when thou dost embrace her.

9 She shall give to thine head an ornament of grace: a crown of glory shall she deliver to thee.

10 Hear, O my son, and receive my sayings; and the years of thy life shall be many.

11 I have taught thee in the way of wisdom; I have led thee in right paths.

12 When thou goest, thy steps shall not be straitened; and when thou runnest, thou shalt not stumble.

13 Take fast hold of instruction; let her not go: keep her; for she is thy life.

14 Enter not into the path of the wicked, and go not in the way of evil men.

15 Avoid it, pass not by it, turn from it, and pass away.

16 For they sleep not, except they have done mischief; and their sleep is taken away, unless they cause some to fall.

17 For they eat the bread of wickedness, and drink the wine of violence.

18 But the path of the just is as the shining light, that shineth more and more unto the perfect day.

19 The way of the wicked is as darkness: they know not at what they stumble.

20 My son, attend to my words; incline thine ear unto my sayings.

21 Let them not depart from thine eyes; keep them in the midst of thine heart.

22 For they are life unto those that find them, and health to all their flesh.

23 Keep thy heart with all diligence; for out of it are the issues of life.

24 Put away from thee a froward mouth, and perverse lips put far from thee.

25 Let thine eyes look right on, and let thine eyelids look straight before thee.

26 Ponder the path of thy feet, and let all thy ways be established.

27 Turn not to the right hand nor to the left: remove thy foot from evil.

Proverbs Chapter 5

My son, attend unto my wisdom, and bow thine ear to my understanding:

2 That thou mayest regard discretion, and that thy lips may keep knowledge.

3 For the lips of a strange woman drop as an honeycomb, and her mouth is smoother than oil:

4 But her end is bitter as wormwood, sharp as a two-edged sword.

5 Her feet go down to death; her steps take hold on hell.

6 Lest thou shouldest ponder the path of life, her ways are moveable, that thou canst not know them.

7 Hear me now therefore, O ye children, and depart not from the words of my mouth.

8 Remove thy way far from her, and come not nigh the door of her house:

9 Lest thou give thine honour unto others, and thy years unto the cruel:

10 Lest strangers be filled with thy wealth; and thy labours be in the house of a stranger;

11 And thou mourn at the last, when thy flesh and thy body are consumed,

12 And say, How have I hated instruction, and my heart despised reproof;

13 And have not obeyed the voice of my teachers, nor inclined mine ear to them that instructed me!

14 I was almost in all evil in the midst of the congregation and assembly.

15 Drink waters out of thine own cistern, and running waters out of thine own well.

16 Let thy fountains be dispersed abroad, and rivers of waters in the streets.

17 Let them be only thine own, and not strangers' with thee.

18 Let thy fountain be blessed: and rejoice with the wife of thy youth.

19 Let her be as the loving hind and pleasant roe; let her breasts satisfy thee at all times; and be thou ravished always with her love.

20 And why wilt thou, my son, be ravished with a strange woman, and embrace the bosom of a stranger?

21 For the ways of man are before the eyes of the Lord, and he pondereth all his goings.

22 His own iniquities shall take the wicked himself, and he shall be holden with the cords of his sins.

23 He shall die without instruction; and in the greatness of his folly he shall go astray.

Proverbs Chapter 6

My son, if thou be surety for thy friend, if thou hast stricken thy hand with a stranger,

2 Thou art snared with the words of thy mouth, thou art taken with the words of thy mouth.

3 Do this now, my son, and deliver thyself, when thou art come into the hand of thy friend; go, humble thyself, and make sure thy friend.

4 Give not sleep to thine eyes, nor slumber to thine eyelids.

5 Deliver thyself as a roe from the hand of the hunter, and as a bird from the hand of the fowler.

6 Go to the ant, thou sluggard; consider her ways, and be wise:

7 Which having no guide, overseer, or ruler,

8 Provideth her meat in the summer, and gathereth her food in the harvest.

9 How long wilt thou sleep, O sluggard? when wilt thou arise out of thy sleep?

10 Yet a little sleep, a little slumber, a little folding of the hands to sleep:

11 So shall thy poverty come as one that travelleth, and thy want as an armed man.

12 A naughty person, a wicked man, walketh with a froward mouth.

13 He winketh with his eyes, he speaketh with his feet, he teacheth with his fingers;

14 Frowardness is in his heart, he deviseth mischief continually; he soweth discord.

15 Therefore shall his calamity come suddenly; suddenly shall he be broken without remedy.

16 These six things doth the Lord hate: yea, seven are an abomination unto him:

17 A proud look, a lying tongue, and hands that shed innocent blood,

18 An heart that deviseth wicked imaginations, feet that be swift in running to mischief,

19 A false witness that speaketh lies, and he that soweth discord among brethren.

20 My son, keep thy father's commandment, and forsake not the law of thy mother:

21 Bind them continually upon thine heart, and tie them about thy neck.

22 When thou goest, it shall lead thee; when thou sleepest, it shall keep thee; and when thou awakest, it shall talk with thee.

23 For the commandment is a lamp; and the law is light; and reproofs of instruction are the way of life:

24 To keep thee from the evil woman, from the flattery of the tongue of a strange woman.

25 Lust not after her beauty in thine heart; neither let her take thee with her eyelids.

26 For by means of a whorish woman a man is brought to a piece of bread: and the adultress will hunt for the precious life.

27 Can a man take fire in his bosom, and his clothes not be burned?

28 Can one go upon hot coals, and his feet not be burned?

29 So he that goeth in to his neighbour's wife; whosoever toucheth her shall not be innocent.

30 Men do not despise a thief, if he steal to satisfy his soul when he is hungry;

31 But if he be found, he shall restore sevenfold; he shall give all the substance of his house.

32 But whoso committeth adultery with a woman lacketh understanding: he that doeth it destroyeth his own soul.

33 A wound and dishonour shall he get; and his reproach shall not be wiped away.

34 For jealousy is the rage of a man: therefore he will not spare in the day of vengeance.

35 He will not regard any ransom; neither will he rest content, though thou givest many gifts.

Proverbs Chapter 7

My son, keep my words, and lay up my commandments with thee.

2 Keep my commandments, and live; and my law as the apple of thine eye.

3 Bind them upon thy fingers, write them upon the table of thine heart.

4 Say unto wisdom, Thou art my sister; and call understanding thy kinswoman:

5 That they may keep thee from the strange woman, from the stranger which flattereth with her words.

6 For at the window of my house I looked through my casement,

7 And beheld among the simple ones, I discerned among the youths, a young man void of understanding,

8 Passing through the street near her corner; and he went the way to her house,

9 In the twilight, in the evening, in the black and dark night:

10 And, behold, there met him a woman with the attire of an harlot, and subtil of heart.

11 (She is loud and stubborn; her feet abide not in her house:

12 Now is she without, now in the streets, and lieth in wait at every corner.)

13 So she caught him, and kissed him, and with an impudent face said unto him,

14 I have peace offerings with me; this day have I payed my vows.

15 Therefore came I forth to meet thee, diligently to seek thy face, and I have found thee.

16 I have decked my bed with coverings of tapestry, with carved works, with fine linen of Egypt.

17 I have perfumed my bed with myrrh, aloes, and cinnamon.

18 Come, let us take our fill of love until the morning: let us solace ourselves with loves.

19 For the goodman is not at home, he is gone a long journey:

20 He hath taken a bag of money with him, and will come home at the day appointed.

21 With her much fair speech she caused him to yield, with the flattering of her lips she forced him.

22 He goeth after her straightway, as an ox goeth to the slaughter, or as a fool to the correction of the stocks;

23 Till a dart strike through his liver; as a bird hasteth to the snare, and knoweth not that it is for his life.

24 Hearken unto me now therefore, O ye children, and attend to the words of my mouth.

25 Let not thine heart decline to her ways, go not astray in her paths.

26 For she hath cast down many wounded: yea, many strong men have been slain by her.

27 Her house is the way to hell, going down to the chambers of death.

Proverbs Chapter 8

Doth not wisdom cry? and understanding put forth her voice?

2 She standeth in the top of high places, by the way in the places of the paths.

3 She crieth at the gates, at the entry of the city, at the coming in at the doors.

4 Unto you, O men, I call; and my voice is to the sons of man.

5 O ye simple, understand wisdom: and, ye fools, be ye of an understanding heart.

6 Hear; for I will speak of excellent things; and the opening of my lips shall be right things.

7 For my mouth shall speak truth; and wickedness is an abomination to my lips.

8 All the words of my mouth are in righteousness; there is nothing froward or perverse in them.

9 They are all plain to him that understandeth, and right to them that find knowledge.

10 Receive my instruction, and not silver; and knowledge rather than choice gold.

11 For wisdom is better than rubies; and all the things that may be desired are not to be compared to it.

12 I wisdom dwell with prudence, and find out knowledge of witty inventions.

13 The fear of the Lord is to hate evil: pride, and arrogancy, and the evil way, and the froward mouth, do I hate.

14 Counsel is mine, and sound wisdom: I am understanding; I have strength.

15 By me kings reign, and princes decree justice.

16 By me princes rule, and nobles, even all the judges of the earth.

17 I love them that love me; and those that seek me early shall find me.

18 Riches and honour are with me; yea, durable riches and righteousness.

19 My fruit is better than gold, yea, than fine gold; and my revenue than choice silver.

20 I lead in the way of righteousness, in the midst of the paths of judgment:

21 That I may cause those that love me to inherit substance; and I will fill their treasures.

22 The Lord possessed me in the beginning of his way, before his works of old.

23 I was set up from everlasting, from the beginning, or ever the earth was.

24 When there were no depths, I was brought forth; when there were no fountains abounding with water.

25 Before the mountains were settled, before the hills was I brought forth:

26 While as yet he had not made the earth, nor the fields, nor the highest part of the dust of the world.

27 When he prepared the heavens, I was there: when he set a compass upon the face of the depth:

28 When he established the clouds above: when he strengthened the fountains of the deep:

29 When he gave to the sea his decree, that the waters should not pass his commandment: when he appointed the foundations of the earth:

30 Then I was by him, as one brought up with him: and I was daily his delight, rejoicing always before him;

31 Rejoicing in the habitable part of his earth; and my delights were with the sons of men.

32 Now therefore hearken unto me, O ye children: for blessed are they that keep my ways.

33 Hear instruction, and be wise, and refuse it not.

34 Blessed is the man that heareth me, watching daily at my gates, waiting at the posts of my doors.

35 For whoso findeth me findeth life, and shall obtain favour of the Lord.

36 But he that sinneth against me wrongeth his own soul: all they that hate me love death.

Proverbs Chapter 9

Wisdom hath builded her house, she hath hewn out her seven pillars:

2 She hath killed her beasts; she hath mingled her wine; she hath also furnished her table.

3 She hath sent forth her maidens: she crieth upon the highest places of the city,

4 Whoso is simple, let him turn in hither: as for him that wanteth understanding, she saith to him,

5 Come, eat of my bread, and drink of the wine which I have mingled.

6 Forsake the foolish, and live; and go in the way of understanding.

7 He that reproveth a scorner getteth to himself shame: and he that rebuketh a wicked man getteth himself a blot.

8 Reprove not a scorner, lest he hate thee: rebuke a wise man, and he will love thee.

9 Give instruction to a wise man, and he will be yet wiser: teach a just man, and he will increase in learning.

10 The fear of the Lord is the beginning of wisdom: and the knowledge of the holy is understanding.

11 For by me thy days shall be multiplied, and the years of thy life shall be increased.

12 If thou be wise, thou shalt be wise for thyself: but if thou scornest, thou alone shalt bear it.

13 A foolish woman is clamorous: she is simple, and knoweth nothing.

14 For she sitteth at the door of her house, on a seat in the high places of the city,

15 To call passengers who go right on their ways:

16 Whoso is simple, let him turn in hither: and as for him that wanteth understanding, she saith to him,

17 Stolen waters are sweet, and bread eaten in secret is pleasant.

18 But he knoweth not that the dead are there; and that her guests are in the depths of hell.

Proverbs Chapter 10

The proverbs of Solomon. A wise son maketh a glad father: but a foolish son is the heaviness of his mother.

2 Treasures of wickedness profit nothing: but righteousness delivereth from death.

3 The Lord will not suffer the soul of the righteous to famish: but he casteth away the substance of the wicked.

4 He becometh poor that dealeth with a slack hand: but the hand of the diligent maketh rich.

5 He that gathereth in summer is a wise son: but he that sleepeth in harvest is a son that causeth shame.

6 Blessings are upon the head of the just: but violence covereth the mouth of the wicked.

7 The memory of the just is blessed: but the name of the wicked shall rot.

8 The wise in heart will receive commandments: but a prating fool shall fall.

9 He that walketh uprightly walketh surely: but he that perverteth his ways shall be known.

10 He that winketh with the eye causeth sorrow: but a prating fool shall fall.

11 The mouth of a righteous man is a well of life: but violence covereth the mouth of the wicked.

12 Hatred stirreth up strifes: but love covereth all sins.

13 In the lips of him that hath understanding wisdom is found: but a rod is for the back of him that is void of understanding.

14 Wise men lay up knowledge: but the mouth of the foolish is near destruction.

15 The rich man's wealth is his strong city: the destruction of the poor is their poverty.

16 The labour of the righteous tendeth to life: the fruit of the wicked to sin.

17 He is in the way of life that keepeth instruction: but he that refuseth reproof erreth.

18 He that hideth hatred with lying lips, and he that uttereth a slander, is a fool.

19 In the multitude of words there wanteth not sin: but he that refraineth his lips is wise.

20 The tongue of the just is as choice silver: the heart of the wicked is little worth.

21 The lips of the righteous feed many: but fools die for want of wisdom.

22 The blessing of the Lord, it maketh rich, and he addeth no sorrow with it.

23 It is as sport to a fool to do mischief: but a man of understanding hath wisdom.

24 The fear of the wicked, it shall come upon him: but the desire of the righteous shall be granted.

25 As the whirlwind passeth, so is the wicked no more: but the righteous is an everlasting foundation.

26 As vinegar to the teeth, and as smoke to the eyes, so is the sluggard to them that send him.

27 The fear of the Lord prolongeth days: but the years of the wicked shall be shortened.

28 The hope of the righteous shall be gladness: but the expectation of the wicked shall perish.

29 The way of the Lord is strength to the upright: but destruction shall be to the workers of iniquity.

30 The righteous shall never be removed: but the wicked shall not inhabit the earth.

31 The mouth of the just bringeth forth wisdom: but the froward tongue shall be cut out.

32 The lips of the righteous know what is acceptable: but the mouth of the wicked speaketh frowardness.

Proverbs Chapter 11

A false balance is abomination to the Lord: but a just weight is his delight.

2 When pride cometh, then cometh shame: but with the lowly is wisdom.

3 The integrity of the upright shall guide them: but the perverseness of transgressors shall destroy them.

4 Riches profit not in the day of wrath: but righteousness delivereth from death.

5 The righteousness of the perfect shall direct his way: but the wicked shall fall by his own wickedness.

6 The righteousness of the upright shall deliver them: but transgressors shall be taken in their own naughtiness.

7 When a wicked man dieth, his expectation shall perish: and the hope of unjust men perisheth.

8 The righteous is delivered out of trouble, and the wicked cometh in his stead.

9 An hypocrite with his mouth destroyeth his neighbour: but through knowledge shall the just be delivered.

10 When it goeth well with the righteous, the city rejoiceth: and when the wicked perish, there is shouting.

11 By the blessing of the upright the city is exalted: but it is overthrown by the mouth of the wicked.

12 He that is void of wisdom despiseth his neighbour: but a man of understanding holdeth his peace.

13 A talebearer revealeth secrets: but he that is of a faithful spirit concealeth the matter.

14 Where no counsel is, the people fall: but in the multitude of counsellors there is safety.

15 He that is surety for a stranger shall smart for it: and he that hateth suretiship is sure.

16 A gracious woman retaineth honour: and strong men retain riches.

17 The merciful man doeth good to his own soul: but he that is cruel troubleth his own flesh.

18 The wicked worketh a deceitful work: but to him that soweth righteousness shall be a sure reward.

19 As righteousness tendeth to life: so he that pursueth evil pursueth it to his own death.

20 They that are of a froward heart are abomination to the Lord: but such as are upright in their way are his delight.

21 Though hand join in hand, the wicked shall not be unpunished: but the seed of the righteous shall be delivered.

22 As a jewel of gold in a swine's snout, so is a fair woman which is without discretion.

23 The desire of the righteous is only good: but the expectation of the wicked is wrath.

24 There is that scattereth, and yet increaseth; and there is that withholdeth more than is meet, but it tendeth to poverty.

25 The liberal soul shall be made fat: and he that watereth shall be watered also himself.

26 He that withholdeth corn, the people shall curse him: but blessing shall be upon the head of him that selleth it.

27 He that diligently seeketh good procureth favour: but he that seeketh mischief, it shall come unto him.

28 He that trusteth in his riches shall fall; but the righteous shall flourish as a branch.

29 He that troubleth his own house shall inherit the wind: and the fool shall be servant to the wise of heart.

30 The fruit of the righteous is a tree of life; and he that winneth souls is wise.

31 Behold, the righteous shall be recompensed in the earth: much more the wicked and the sinner.

Proverbs Chapter 12

Whoso loveth instruction loveth knowledge: but he that hateth reproof is brutish.

2 A good man obtaineth favour of the Lord: but a man of wicked devices will he condemn.

3 A man shall not be established by wickedness: but the root of the righteous shall not be moved.

4 A virtuous woman is a crown to her husband: but she that maketh ashamed is as rottenness in his bones.

5 The thoughts of the righteous are right: but the counsels of the wicked are deceit.

6 The words of the wicked are to lie in wait for blood: but the mouth of the upright shall deliver them.

7 The wicked are overthrown, and are not: but the house of the righteous shall stand.

8 A man shall be commended according to his wisdom: but he that is of a perverse heart shall be despised.

9 He that is despised, and hath a servant, is better than he that honoureth himself, and lacketh bread.

10 A righteous man regardeth the life of his beast: but the tender mercies of the wicked are cruel.

11 He that tilleth his land shall be satisfied with bread: but he that followeth vain persons is void of understanding.

12 The wicked desireth the net of evil men: but the root of the righteous yieldeth fruit.

13 The wicked is snared by the transgression of his lips: but the just shall come out of trouble.

14 A man shall be satisfied with good by the fruit of his mouth: and the recompence of a man's hands shall be rendered unto him.

15 The way of a fool is right in his own eyes: but he that hearkeneth unto counsel is wise.

16 A fool's wrath is presently known: but a prudent man covereth shame.

17 He that speaketh truth sheweth forth righteousness: but a false witness deceit.

18 There is that speaketh like the piercings of a sword: but the tongue of the wise is health.

19 The lip of truth shall be established for ever: but a lying tongue is but for a moment.

20 Deceit is in the heart of them that imagine evil: but to the counsellors of peace is joy.

21 There shall no evil happen to the just: but the wicked shall be filled with mischief.

22 Lying lips are abomination to the Lord: but they that deal truly are his delight.

23 A prudent man concealeth knowledge: but the heart of fools proclaimeth foolishness.

24 The hand of the diligent shall bear rule: but the slothful shall be under tribute.

25 Heaviness in the heart of man maketh it stoop: but a good word maketh it glad.

26 The righteous is more excellent than his neighbour: but the way of the wicked seduceth them.

27 The slothful man roasteth not that which he took in hunting: but the substance of a diligent man is precious.

28 In the way of righteousness is life: and in the pathway thereof there is no death.

Proverbs Chapter 13

A wise son heareth his father's instruction: but a scorner heareth not rebuke.

2 A man shall eat good by the fruit of his mouth: but the soul of the transgressors shall eat violence.

3 He that keepeth his mouth keepeth his life: but he that openeth wide his lips shall have destruction.

4 The soul of the sluggard desireth, and hath nothing: but the soul of the diligent shall be made fat.

5 A righteous man hateth lying: but a wicked man is loathsome, and cometh to shame.

6 Righteousness keepeth him that is upright in the way: but wickedness overthroweth the sinner.

7 There is that maketh himself rich, yet hath nothing: there is that maketh himself poor, yet hath great riches.

8 The ransom of a man's life are his riches: but the poor heareth not rebuke.

9 The light of the righteous rejoiceth: but the lamp of the wicked shall be put out.

10 Only by pride cometh contention: but with the well advised is wisdom.

11 Wealth gotten by vanity shall be diminished: but he that gathereth by labour shall increase.

12 Hope deferred maketh the heart sick: but when the desire cometh, it is a tree of life.

13 Whoso despiseth the word shall be destroyed: but he that feareth the commandment shall be rewarded.

14 The law of the wise is a fountain of life, to depart from the snares of death.

15 Good understanding giveth favour: but the way of transgressors is hard.

16 Every prudent man dealeth with knowledge: but a fool layeth open his folly.

17 A wicked messenger falleth into mischief: but a faithful ambassador is health.

18 Poverty and shame shall be to him that refuseth instruction: but he that regardeth reproof shall be honoured.

19 The desire accomplished is sweet to the soul: but it is abomination to fools to depart from evil.

20 He that walketh with wise men shall be wise: but a companion of fools shall be destroyed.

21 Evil pursueth sinners: but to the righteous good shall be repayed.

22 A good man leaveth an inheritance to his children's children: and the wealth of the sinner is laid up for the just.

23 Much food is in the tillage of the poor: but there is that is destroyed for want of judgment.

24 He that spareth his rod hateth his son: but he that loveth him chasteneth him betimes.

25 The righteous eateth to the satisfying of his soul: but the belly of the wicked shall want.

Proverbs Chapter 14

Every wise woman buildeth her house: but the foolish plucketh it down with her hands.

2 He that walketh in his uprightness feareth the Lord: but he that is perverse in his ways despiseth him.

3 In the mouth of the foolish is a rod of pride: but the lips of the wise shall preserve them.

4 Where no oxen are, the crib is clean: but much increase is by the strength of the ox.

5 A faithful witness will not lie: but a false witness will utter lies.

6 A scorner seeketh wisdom, and findeth it not: but knowledge is easy unto him that understandeth.

7 Go from the presence of a foolish man, when thou perceivest not in him the lips of knowledge.

8 The wisdom of the prudent is to understand his way: but the folly of fools is deceit.

9 Fools make a mock at sin: but among the righteous there is favour.

10 The heart knoweth his own bitterness; and a stranger doth not intermeddle with his joy.

11 The house of the wicked shall be overthrown: but the tabernacle of the upright shall flourish.

12 There is a way which seemeth right unto a man, but the end thereof are the ways of death.

13 Even in laughter the heart is sorrowful; and the end of that mirth is heaviness.

14 The backslider in heart shall be filled with his own ways: and a good man shall be satisfied from himself.

15 The simple believeth every word: but the prudent man looketh well to his going.

16 A wise man feareth, and departeth from evil: but the fool rageth, and is confident.

17 He that is soon angry dealeth foolishly: and a man of wicked devices is hated.

18 The simple inherit folly: but the prudent are crowned with knowledge.

19 The evil bow before the good; and the wicked at the gates of the righteous.

20 The poor is hated even of his own neighbour: but the rich hath many friends.

21 He that despiseth his neighbour sinneth: but he that hath mercy on the poor, happy is he.

22 Do they not err that devise evil? but mercy and truth shall be to them that devise good.

23 In all labour there is profit: but the talk of the lips tendeth only to penury.

24 The crown of the wise is their riches: but the foolishness of fools is folly.

25 A true witness delivereth souls: but a deceitful witness speaketh lies.

26 In the fear of the Lord is strong confidence: and his children shall have a place of refuge.

27 The fear of the Lord is a fountain of life, to depart from the snares of death.

28 In the multitude of people is the king's honour: but in the want of people is the destruction of the prince.

29 He that is slow to wrath is of great understanding: but he that is hasty of spirit exalteth folly.

30 A sound heart is the life of the flesh: but envy the rottenness of the bones.

31 He that oppresseth the poor reproacheth his Maker: but he that honoureth him hath mercy on the poor.

32 The wicked is driven away in his wickedness: but the righteous hath hope in his death.

33 Wisdom resteth in the heart of him that hath understanding: but that which is in the midst of fools is made known.

34 Righteousness exalteth a nation: but sin is a reproach to any people.

35 The king's favour is toward a wise servant: but his wrath is against him that causeth shame.

Proverbs Chapter 15

A soft answer turneth away wrath: but grievous words stir up anger.

2 The tongue of the wise useth knowledge aright: but the mouth of fools poureth out foolishness.

3 The eyes of the Lord are in every place, beholding the evil and the good.

4 A wholesome tongue is a tree of life: but perverseness therein is a breach in the spirit.

5 A fool despiseth his father's instruction: but he that regardeth reproof is prudent.

6 In the house of the righteous is much treasure: but in the revenues of the wicked is trouble.

7 The lips of the wise disperse knowledge: but the heart of the foolish doeth not so.

8 The sacrifice of the wicked is an abomination to the Lord: but the prayer of the upright is his delight.

9 The way of the wicked is an abomination unto the Lord: but he loveth him that followeth after righteousness.

10 Correction is grievous unto him that forsaketh the way: and he that hateth reproof shall die.

11 Hell and destruction are before the Lord: how much more then the hearts of the children of men?

12 A scorner loveth not one that reproveth him: neither will he go unto the wise.

13 A merry heart maketh a cheerful countenance: but by sorrow of the heart the spirit is broken.

14 The heart of him that hath understanding seeketh knowledge: but the mouth of fools feedeth on foolishness.

15 All the days of the afflicted are evil: but he that is of a merry heart hath a continual feast.

16 Better is little with the fear of the Lord than great treasure and trouble therewith.

17 Better is a dinner of herbs where love is, than a stalled ox and hatred therewith.

18 A wrathful man stirreth up strife: but he that is slow to anger appeaseth strife.

19 The way of the slothful man is as an hedge of thorns: but the way of the righteous is made plain.

20 A wise son maketh a glad father: but a foolish man despiseth his mother.

21 Folly is joy to him that is destitute of wisdom: but a man of understanding walketh uprightly.

22 Without counsel purposes are disappointed: but in the multitude of counsellors they are established.

23 A man hath joy by the answer of his mouth: and a word spoken in due season, how good is it!

24 The way of life is above to the wise, that he may depart from hell beneath.

25 The Lord will destroy the house of the proud: but he will establish the border of the widow.

26 The thoughts of the wicked are an abomination to the Lord: but the words of the pure are pleasant words.

27 He that is greedy of gain troubleth his own house; but he that hateth gifts shall live.

28 The heart of the righteous studieth to answer: but the mouth of the wicked poureth out evil things.

29 The Lord is far from the wicked: but he heareth the prayer of the righteous.

30 The light of the eyes rejoiceth the heart: and a good report maketh the bones fat.

31 The ear that heareth the reproof of life abideth among the wise.

32 He that refuseth instruction despiseth his own soul: but he that heareth reproof getteth understanding.

33 The fear of the Lord is the instruction of wisdom; and before honour is humility.

Proverbs Chapter 16

The preparations of the heart in man, and the answer of the tongue, is from the Lord.

2 All the ways of a man are clean in his own eyes; but the Lord weigheth the spirits.

3 Commit thy works unto the Lord, and thy thoughts shall be established.

4 The Lord hath made all things for himself: yea, even the wicked for the day of evil.

5 Every one that is proud in heart is an abomination to the Lord: though hand join in hand, he shall not be unpunished.

6 By mercy and truth iniquity is purged: and by the fear of the Lord men depart from evil.

7 When a man's ways please the Lord, he maketh even his enemies to be at peace with him.

8 Better is a little with righteousness than great revenues without right.

9 A man's heart deviseth his way: but the Lord directeth his steps.

10 A divine sentence is in the lips of the king: his mouth transgresseth not in judgment.

11 A just weight and balance are the Lord's: all the weights of the bag are his work.

12 It is an abomination to kings to commit wickedness: for the throne is established by righteousness.

13 Righteous lips are the delight of kings; and they love him that speaketh right.

14 The wrath of a king is as messengers of death: but a wise man will pacify it.

15 In the light of the king's countenance is life; and his favour is as a cloud of the latter rain.

16 How much better is it to get wisdom than gold! and to get understanding rather to be chosen than silver!

17 The highway of the upright is to depart from evil: he that keepeth his way preserveth his soul.

18 Pride goeth before destruction, and an haughty spirit before a fall.

19 Better it is to be of an humble spirit with the lowly, than to divide the spoil with the proud.

20 He that handleth a matter wisely shall find good: and whoso trusteth in the Lord, happy is he.

21 The wise in heart shall be called prudent: and the sweetness of the lips increaseth learning.

22 Understanding is a wellspring of life unto him that hath it: but the instruction of fools is folly.

23 The heart of the wise teacheth his mouth, and addeth learning to his lips.

24 Pleasant words are as an honeycomb, sweet to the soul, and health to the bones.

25 There is a way that seemeth right unto a man, but the end thereof are the ways of death.

26 He that laboureth laboureth for himself; for his mouth craveth it of him.

27 An ungodly man diggeth up evil: and in his lips there is as a burning fire.

28 A froward man soweth strife: and a whisperer separateth chief friends.

29 A violent man enticeth his neighbour, and leadeth him into the way that is not good.

30 He shutteth his eyes to devise froward things: moving his lips he bringeth evil to pass.

31 The hoary head is a crown of glory, if it be found in the way of righteousness.

32 He that is slow to anger is better than the mighty; and he that ruleth his spirit than he that taketh a city.

33 The lot is cast into the lap; but the whole disposing thereof is of the Lord.

Proverbs Chapter 17

Better is a dry morsel, and quietness therewith, than an house full of sacrifices with strife.

2 A wise servant shall have rule over a son that causeth shame, and shall have part of the inheritance among the brethren.

3 The fining pot is for silver, and the furnace for gold: but the Lord trieth the hearts.

4 A wicked doer giveth heed to false lips; and a liar giveth ear to a naughty tongue.

5 Whoso mocketh the poor reproacheth his Maker: and he that is glad at calamities shall not be unpunished.

6 Children's children are the crown of old men; and the glory of children are their fathers.

7 Excellent speech becometh not a fool: much less do lying lips a prince.

8 A gift is as a precious stone in the eyes of him that hath it: whithersoever it turneth, it prospereth.

9 He that covereth a transgression seeketh love; but he that repeateth a matter separateth very friends.

10 A reproof entereth more into a wise man than an hundred stripes into a fool.

11 An evil man seeketh only rebellion: therefore a cruel messenger shall be sent against him.

12 Let a bear robbed of her whelps meet a man, rather than a fool in his folly.

13 Whoso rewardeth evil for good, evil shall not depart from his house.

14 The beginning of strife is as when one letteth out water: therefore leave off contention, before it be meddled with.

15 He that justifieth the wicked, and he that condemneth the just, even they both are abomination to the Lord.

16 Wherefore is there a price in the hand of a fool to get wisdom, seeing he hath no heart to it?

17 A friend loveth at all times, and a brother is born for adversity.

18 A man void of understanding striketh hands, and becometh surety in the presence of his friend.

19 He loveth transgression that loveth strife: and he that exalteth his gate seeketh destruction.

20 He that hath a froward heart findeth no good: and he that hath a perverse tongue falleth into mischief.

21 He that begetteth a fool doeth it to his sorrow: and the father of a fool hath no joy.

22 A merry heart doeth good like a medicine: but a broken spirit drieth the bones.

23 A wicked man taketh a gift out of the bosom to pervert the ways of judgment.

24 Wisdom is before him that hath understanding; but the eyes of a fool are in the ends of the earth.

25 A foolish son is a grief to his father, and bitterness to her that bare him.

26 Also to punish the just is not good, nor to strike princes for equity.

27 He that hath knowledge spareth his words: and a man of understanding is of an excellent spirit.

28 Even a fool, when he holdeth his peace, is counted wise: and he that shutteth his lips is esteemed a man of understanding.

Proverbs Chapter 18

Through desire a man, having separated himself, seeketh and intermeddleth with all wisdom.

2 A fool hath no delight in understanding, but that his heart may discover itself.

3 When the wicked cometh, then cometh also contempt, and with ignominy reproach.

4 The words of a man's mouth are as deep waters, and the wellspring of wisdom as a flowing brook.

5 It is not good to accept the person of the wicked, to overthrow the righteous in judgment.

6 A fool's lips enter into contention, and his mouth calleth for strokes.

7 A fool's mouth is his destruction, and his lips are the snare of his soul.

8 The words of a talebearer are as wounds, and they go down into the innermost parts of the belly.

9 He also that is slothful in his work is brother to him that is a great waster.

10 The name of the Lord is a strong tower: the righteous runneth into it, and is safe.

11 The rich man's wealth is his strong city, and as an high wall in his own conceit.

12 Before destruction the heart of man is haughty, and before honour is humility.

13 He that answereth a matter before he heareth it, it is folly and shame unto him.

14 The spirit of a man will sustain his infirmity; but a wounded spirit who can bear?

15 The heart of the prudent getteth knowledge; and the ear of the wise seeketh knowledge.

16 A man's gift maketh room for him, and bringeth him before great men.

17 He that is first in his own cause seemeth just; but his neighbour cometh and searcheth him.

18 The lot causeth contentions to cease, and parteth between the mighty.

19 A brother offended is harder to be won than a strong city: and their contentions are like the bars of a castle.

20 A man's belly shall be satisfied with the fruit of his mouth; and with the increase of his lips shall he be filled.

21 Death and life are in the power of the tongue: and they that love it shall eat the fruit thereof.

22 Whoso findeth a wife findeth a good thing, and obtaineth favour of the Lord.

23 The poor useth intreaties; but the rich answereth roughly.

24 A man that hath friends must shew himself friendly: and there is a friend that sticketh closer than a brother.

Proverbs Chapter 19

Better is the poor that walketh in his integrity, than he that is perverse in his lips, and is a fool.

2 Also, that the soul be without knowledge, it is not good; and he that hasteth with his feet sinneth.

3 The foolishness of man perverteth his way: and his heart fretteth against the Lord.

4 Wealth maketh many friends; but the poor is separated from his neighbour.

5 A false witness shall not be unpunished, and he that speaketh lies shall not escape.

6 Many will intreat the favour of the prince: and every man is a friend to him that giveth gifts.

7 All the brethren of the poor do hate him: how much more do his friends go far from him? he pursueth them with words, yet they are wanting to him.

8 He that getteth wisdom loveth his own soul: he that keepeth understanding shall find good.

9 A false witness shall not be unpunished, and he that speaketh lies shall perish.

10 Delight is not seemly for a fool; much less for a servant to have rule over princes.

11 The discretion of a man deferreth his anger; and it is his glory to pass over a transgression.

12 The king's wrath is as the roaring of a lion; but his favour is as dew upon the grass.

13 A foolish son is the calamity of his father: and the contentions of a wife are a continual dropping.

14 House and riches are the inheritance of fathers: and a prudent wife is from the Lord.

15 Slothfulness casteth into a deep sleep; and an idle soul shall suffer hunger.

16 He that keepeth the commandment keepeth his own soul; but he that despiseth his ways shall die.

17 He that hath pity upon the poor lendeth unto the Lord; and that which he hath given will he pay him again.

18 Chasten thy son while there is hope, and let not thy soul spare for his crying.

19 A man of great wrath shall suffer punishment: for if thou deliver him, yet thou must do it again.

20 Hear counsel, and receive instruction, that thou mayest be wise in thy latter end.

21 There are many devices in a man's heart; nevertheless the counsel of the Lord, that shall stand.

22 The desire of a man is his kindness: and a poor man is better than a liar.

23 The fear of the Lord tendeth to life: and he that hath it shall abide satisfied; he shall not be visited with evil.

24 A slothful man hideth his hand in his bosom, and will not so much as bring it to his mouth again.

25 Smite a scorner, and the simple will beware: and reprove one that hath understanding, and he will understand knowledge.

26 He that wasteth his father, and chaseth away his mother, is a son that causeth shame, and bringeth reproach.

27 Cease, my son, to hear the instruction that causeth to err from the words of knowledge.

28 An ungodly witness scorneth judgment: and the mouth of the wicked devoureth iniquity.

29 Judgments are prepared for scorners, and stripes for the back of fools.

Proverbs Chapter 20

Wine is a mocker, strong drink is raging: and whosoever is deceived thereby is not wise.

2 The fear of a king is as the roaring of a lion: whoso provoketh him to anger sinneth against his own soul.

3 It is an honour for a man to cease from strife: but every fool will be meddling.

4 The sluggard will not plow by reason of the cold; therefore shall he beg in harvest, and have nothing.

5 Counsel in the heart of man is like deep water; but a man of understanding will draw it out.

6 Most men will proclaim every one his own goodness: but a faithful man who can find?

7 The just man walketh in his integrity: his children are blessed after him.

8 A king that sitteth in the throne of judgment scattereth away all evil with his eyes.

9 Who can say, I have made my heart clean, I am pure from my sin?

10 Divers weights, and divers measures, both of them are alike abomination to the Lord.

11 Even a child is known by his doings, whether his work be pure, and whether it be right.

12 The hearing ear, and the seeing eye, the Lord hath made even both of them.

13 Love not sleep, lest thou come to poverty; open thine eyes, and thou shalt be satisfied with bread.

14 It is naught, it is naught, saith the buyer: but when he is gone his way, then he boasteth.

15 There is gold, and a multitude of rubies: but the lips of knowledge are a precious jewel.

16 Take his garment that is surety for a stranger: and take a pledge of him for a strange woman.

17 Bread of deceit is sweet to a man; but afterwards his mouth shall be filled with gravel.

18 Every purpose is established by counsel: and with good advice make war.

19 He that goeth about as a talebearer revealeth secrets: therefore meddle not with him that flattereth with his lips.

20 Whoso curseth his father or his mother, his lamp shall be put out in obscure darkness.

21 An inheritance may be gotten hastily at the beginning; but the end thereof shall not be blessed.

22 Say not thou, I will recompense evil; but wait on the Lord, and he shall save thee.

23 Divers weights are an abomination unto the Lord; and a false balance is not good.

24 Man's goings are of the Lord; how can a man then understand his own way?

25 It is a snare to the man who devoureth that which is holy, and after vows to make enquiry.

26 A wise king scattereth the wicked, and bringeth the wheel over them.

27 The spirit of man is the candle of the Lord, searching all the inward parts of the belly.

28 Mercy and truth preserve the king: and his throne is upholden by mercy.

29 The glory of young men is their strength: and the beauty of old men is the grey head.

30 The blueness of a wound cleanseth away evil: so do stripes the inward parts of the belly.

Proverbs Chapter 21

The king's heart is in the hand of the Lord, as the rivers of water: he turneth it whithersoever he will.

2 Every way of a man is right in his own eyes: but the Lord pondereth the hearts.

3 To do justice and judgment is more acceptable to the Lord than sacrifice.

4 An high look, and a proud heart, and the plowing of the wicked, is sin.

5 The thoughts of the diligent tend only to plenteousness; but of every one that is hasty only to want.

6 The getting of treasures by a lying tongue is a vanity tossed to and fro of them that seek death.

7 The robbery of the wicked shall destroy them; because they refuse to do judgment.

8 The way of man is froward and strange: but as for the pure, his work is right.

9 It is better to dwell in a corner of the housetop, than with a brawling woman in a wide house.

10 The soul of the wicked desireth evil: his neighbour findeth no favour in his eyes.

11 When the scorner is punished, the simple is made wise: and when the wise is instructed, he receiveth knowledge.

12 The righteous man wisely considereth the house of the wicked: but God overthroweth the wicked for their wickedness.

13 Whoso stoppeth his ears at the cry of the poor, he also shall cry himself, but shall not be heard.

14 A gift in secret pacifieth anger: and a reward in the bosom strong wrath.

15 It is joy to the just to do judgment: but destruction shall be to the workers of iniquity.

16 The man that wandereth out of the way of understanding shall remain in the congregation of the dead.

17 He that loveth pleasure shall be a poor man: he that loveth wine and oil shall not be rich.

18 The wicked shall be a ransom for the righteous, and the transgressor for the upright.

19 It is better to dwell in the wilderness, than with a contentious and an angry woman.

20 There is treasure to be desired and oil in the dwelling of the wise; but a foolish man spendeth it up.

21 He that followeth after righteousness and mercy findeth life, righteousness, and honour.

22 A wise man scaleth the city of the mighty, and casteth down the strength of the confidence thereof.

23 Whoso keepeth his mouth and his tongue keepeth his soul from troubles.

24 Proud and haughty scorner is his name, who dealeth in proud wrath.

25 The desire of the slothful killeth him; for his hands refuse to labour.

26 He coveteth greedily all the day long: but the righteous giveth and spareth not.

27 The sacrifice of the wicked is abomination: how much more, when he bringeth it with a wicked mind?

28 A false witness shall perish: but the man that heareth speaketh constantly.

29 A wicked man hardeneth his face: but as for the upright, he directeth his way.

30 There is no wisdom nor understanding nor counsel against the Lord.

31 The horse is prepared against the day of battle: but safety is of the Lord.

Proverbs Chapter 22

A good name is rather to be chosen than great riches, and loving favour rather than silver and gold.

2 The rich and poor meet together: the Lord is the maker of them all.

3 A prudent man foreseeth the evil, and hideth himself: but the simple pass on, and are punished.

4 By humility and the fear of the Lord are riches, and honour, and life.

5 Thorns and snares are in the way of the froward: he that doth keep his soul shall be far from them.

6 Train up a child in the way he should go: and when he is old, he will not depart from it.

7 The rich ruleth over the poor, and the borrower is servant to the lender.

8 He that soweth iniquity shall reap vanity: and the rod of his anger shall fail.

9 He that hath a bountiful eye shall be blessed; for he giveth of his bread to the poor.

10 Cast out the scorner, and contention shall go out; yea, strife and reproach shall cease.

11 He that loveth pureness of heart, for the grace of his lips the king shall be his friend.

12 The eyes of the Lord preserve knowledge, and he overthroweth the words of the transgressor.

13 The slothful man saith, There is a lion without, I shall be slain in the streets.

14 The mouth of strange women is a deep pit: he that is abhorred of the Lord shall fall therein.

15 Foolishness is bound in the heart of a child; but the rod of correction shall drive it far from him.

16 He that oppresseth the poor to increase his riches, and he that giveth to the rich, shall surely come to want.

17 Bow down thine ear, and hear the words of the wise, and apply thine heart unto my knowledge.

18 For it is a pleasant thing if thou keep them within thee; they shall withal be fitted in thy lips.

19 That thy trust may be in the Lord, I have made known to thee this day, even to thee.

20 Have not I written to thee excellent things in counsels and knowledge,

21 That I might make thee know the certainty of the words of truth; that thou mightest answer the words of truth to them that send unto thee?

22 Rob not the poor, because he is poor: neither oppress the afflicted in the gate:

23 For the Lord will plead their cause, and spoil the soul of those that spoiled them.

24 Make no friendship with an angry man; and with a furious man thou shalt not go:

25 Lest thou learn his ways, and get a snare to thy soul.

26 Be not thou one of them that strike hands, or of them that are sureties for debts.

27 If thou hast nothing to pay, why should he take away thy bed from under thee?

28 Remove not the ancient landmark, which thy fathers have set.

29 Seest thou a man diligent in his business? he shall stand before kings; he shall not stand before mean men.

Proverbs Chapter 23

When thou sittest to eat with a ruler, consider diligently what is before thee:

2 And put a knife to thy throat, if thou be a man given to appetite.

3 Be not desirous of his dainties: for they are deceitful meat.

4 Labour not to be rich: cease from thine own wisdom.

5 Wilt thou set thine eyes upon that which is not? for riches certainly make themselves wings; they fly away as an eagle toward heaven.

6 Eat thou not the bread of him that hath an evil eye, neither desire thou his dainty meats:

7 For as he thinketh in his heart, so is he: Eat and drink, saith he to thee; but his heart is not with thee.

8 The morsel which thou hast eaten shalt thou vomit up, and lose thy sweet words.

9 Speak not in the ears of a fool: for he will despise the wisdom of thy words.

10 Remove not the old landmark; and enter not into the fields of the fatherless:

11 For their redeemer is mighty; he shall plead their cause with thee.

12 Apply thine heart unto instruction, and thine ears to the words of knowledge.

13 Withhold not correction from the child: for if thou beatest him with the rod, he shall not die.

14 Thou shalt beat him with the rod, and shalt deliver his soul from hell.

15 My son, if thine heart be wise, my heart shall rejoice, even mine.

16 Yea, my reins shall rejoice, when thy lips speak right things.

17 Let not thine heart envy sinners: but be thou in the fear of the Lord all the day long.

18 For surely there is an end; and thine expectation shall not be cut off.

19 Hear thou, my son, and be wise, and guide thine heart in the way.

20 Be not among winebibbers; among riotous eaters of flesh:

21 For the drunkard and the glutton shall come to poverty: and drowsiness shall clothe a man with rags.

22 Hearken unto thy father that begat thee, and despise not thy mother when she is old.

23 Buy the truth, and sell it not; also wisdom, and instruction, and understanding.

24 The father of the righteous shall greatly rejoice: and he that begetteth a wise child shall have joy of him.

25 Thy father and thy mother shall be glad, and she that bare thee shall rejoice.

26 My son, give me thine heart, and let thine eyes observe my ways.

27 For a whore is a deep ditch; and a strange woman is a narrow pit.

28 She also lieth in wait as for a prey, and increaseth the transgressors among men.

29 Who hath woe? who hath sorrow? who hath contentions? who hath babbling? who hath wounds without cause? who hath redness of eyes?

30 They that tarry long at the wine; they that go to seek mixed wine.

31 Look not thou upon the wine when it is red, when it giveth his colour in the cup, when it moveth itself aright.

32 At the last it biteth like a serpent, and stingeth like an adder.

33 Thine eyes shall behold strange women, and thine heart shall utter perverse things.

34 Yea, thou shalt be as he that lieth down in the midst of the sea, or as he that lieth upon the top of a mast.

35 They have stricken me, shalt thou say, and I was not sick; they have beaten me, and I felt it not: when shall I awake? I will seek it yet again

Proverbs Chapter 24

Be not thou envious against evil men, neither desire to be with them.

2 For their heart studieth destruction, and their lips talk of mischief.

3 Through wisdom is an house builded; and by understanding it is established:

4 And by knowledge shall the chambers be filled with all precious and pleasant riches.

5 A wise man is strong; yea, a man of knowledge increaseth strength.

6 For by wise counsel thou shalt make thy war: and in multitude of counsellors there is safety.

7 Wisdom is too high for a fool: he openeth not his mouth in the gate.

8 He that deviseth to do evil shall be called a mischievous person.

9 The thought of foolishness is sin: and the scorner is an abomination to men.

10 If thou faint in the day of adversity, thy strength is small.

11 If thou forbear to deliver them that are drawn unto death, and those that are ready to be slain;

12 If thou sayest, Behold, we knew it not; doth not he that pondereth the heart consider it? and he that keepeth thy soul, doth not he know it? and shall not he render to every man according to his works?

13 My son, eat thou honey, because it is good; and the honeycomb, which is sweet to thy taste:

14 So shall the knowledge of wisdom be unto thy soul: when thou hast found it, then there shall be a reward, and thy expectation shall not be cut off.

15 Lay not wait, O wicked man, against the dwelling of the righteous; spoil not his resting place:

16 For a just man falleth seven times, and riseth up again: but the wicked shall fall into mischief.

17 Rejoice not when thine enemy falleth, and let not thine heart be glad when he stumbleth:

18 Lest the Lord see it, and it displease him, and he turn away his wrath from him.

19 Fret not thyself because of evil men, neither be thou envious at the wicked:

20 For there shall be no reward to the evil man; the candle of the wicked shall be put out.

21 My son, fear thou the Lord and the king: and meddle not with them that are given to change:

22 For their calamity shall rise suddenly; and who knoweth the ruin of them both?

23 These things also belong to the wise. It is not good to have respect of persons in judgment.

24 He that saith unto the wicked, Thou are righteous; him shall the people curse, nations shall abhor him:

25 But to them that rebuke him shall be delight, and a good blessing shall come upon them.

26 Every man shall kiss his lips that giveth a right answer.

27 Prepare thy work without, and make it fit for thyself in the field; and afterwards build thine house.

28 Be not a witness against thy neighbour without cause; and deceive not with thy lips.

29 Say not, I will do so to him as he hath done to me: I will render to the man according to his work.

30 I went by the field of the slothful, and by the vineyard of the man void of understanding;

31 And, lo, it was all grown over with thorns, and nettles had covered the face thereof, and the stone wall thereof was broken down.

32 Then I saw, and considered it well: I looked upon it, and received instruction.

33 Yet a little sleep, a little slumber, a little folding of the hands to sleep:

34 So shall thy poverty come as one that travelleth; and thy want as an armed man.

Proverbs Chapter 25

These are also proverbs of Solomon, which the men of Hezekiah king of Judah copied out.

2 It is the glory of God to conceal a thing: but the honour of kings is to search out a matter.

3 The heaven for height, and the earth for depth, and the heart of kings is unsearchable.

4 Take away the dross from the silver, and there shall come forth a vessel for the finer.

5 Take away the wicked from before the king, and his throne shall be established in righteousness.

6 Put not forth thyself in the presence of the king, and stand not in the place of great men:

7 For better it is that it be said unto thee, Come up hither; than that thou shouldest be put lower in the presence of the prince whom thine eyes have seen.

8 Go not forth hastily to strive, lest thou know not what to do in the end thereof, when thy neighbour hath put thee to shame.

9 Debate thy cause with thy neighbour himself; and discover not a secret to another:

10 Lest he that heareth it put thee to shame, and thine infamy turn not away.

11 A word fitly spoken is like apples of gold in pictures of silver.

12 As an earring of gold, and an ornament of fine gold, so is a wise reprover upon an obedient ear.

13 As the cold of snow in the time of harvest, so is a faithful messenger to them that send him: for he refresheth the soul of his masters.

14 Whoso boasteth himself of a false gift is like clouds and wind without rain.

15 By long forbearing is a prince persuaded, and a soft tongue breaketh the bone.

16 Hast thou found honey? eat so much as is sufficient for thee, lest thou be filled therewith, and vomit it.

17 Withdraw thy foot from thy neighbour's house; lest he be weary of thee, and so hate thee.

18 A man that beareth false witness against his neighbour is a maul, and a sword, and a sharp arrow.

19 Confidence in an unfaithful man in time of trouble is like a broken tooth, and a foot out of joint.

20 As he that taketh away a garment in cold weather, and as vinegar upon nitre, so is he that singeth songs to an heavy heart.

21 If thine enemy be hungry, give him bread to eat; and if he be thirsty, give him water to drink:

22 For thou shalt heap coals of fire upon his head, and the Lord shall reward thee.

23 The north wind driveth away rain: so doth an angry countenance a backbiting tongue.

24 It is better to dwell in the corner of the housetop, than with a brawling woman and in a wide house.

25 As cold waters to a thirsty soul, so is good news from a far country.

26 A righteous man falling down before the wicked is as a troubled fountain, and a corrupt spring.

27 It is not good to eat much honey: so for men to search their own glory is not glory.

28 He that hath no rule over his own spirit is like a city that is broken down, and without walls.

As snow in summer, and as rain in harvest, so honour is not seemly for a fool.

2 As the bird by wandering, as the swallow by flying, so the curse causeless shall not come.

3 A whip for the horse, a bridle for the ass, and a rod for the fool's back.

4 Answer not a fool according to his folly, lest thou also be like unto him.

5 Answer a fool according to his folly, lest he be wise in his own conceit.

6 He that sendeth a message by the hand of a fool cutteth off the feet, and drinketh damage.

7 The legs of the lame are not equal: so is a parable in the mouth of fools.

8 As he that bindeth a stone in a sling, so is he that giveth honour to a fool.

9 As a thorn goeth up into the hand of a drunkard, so is a parable in the mouths of fools.

10 The great God that formed all things both rewardeth the fool, and rewardeth transgressors.

11 As a dog returneth to his vomit, so a fool returneth to his folly.

12 Seest thou a man wise in his own conceit? there is more hope of a fool than of him.

13 The slothful man saith, There is a lion in the way; a lion is in the streets.

14 As the door turneth upon his hinges, so doth the slothful upon his bed.

15 The slothful hideth his hand in his bosom; it grieveth him to bring it again to his mouth.

16 The sluggard is wiser in his own conceit than seven men that can render a reason.

17 He that passeth by, and meddleth with strife belonging not to him, is like one that taketh a dog by the ears.

18 As a mad man who casteth firebrands, arrows, and death,

19 So is the man that deceiveth his neighbour, and saith, Am not I in sport?

20 Where no wood is, there the fire goeth out: so where there is no talebearer, the strife ceaseth.

21 As coals are to burning coals, and wood to fire; so is a contentious man to kindle strife.

22 The words of a talebearer are as wounds, and they go down into the innermost parts of the belly.

23 Burning lips and a wicked heart are like a potsherd covered with silver dross.

24 He that hateth dissembleth with his lips, and layeth up deceit within him;

25 When he speaketh fair, believe him not: for there are seven abominations in his heart.

26 Whose hatred is covered by deceit, his wickedness shall be shewed before the whole congregation.

27 Whoso diggeth a pit shall fall therein: and he that rolleth a stone, it will return upon him.

28 A lying tongue hateth those that are afflicted by it; and a flattering mouth worketh ruin.

Proverbs Chapter 27

Boast not thyself of to morrow; for thou knowest not what a day may bring forth.

2 Let another man praise thee, and not thine own mouth; a stranger, and not thine own lips.

3 A stone is heavy, and the sand weighty; but a fool's wrath is heavier than them both.

4 Wrath is cruel, and anger is outrageous; but who is able to stand before envy?

5 Open rebuke is better than secret love.

6 Faithful are the wounds of a friend; but the kisses of an enemy are deceitful.

7 The full soul loatheth an honeycomb; but to the hungry soul every bitter thing is sweet.

8 As a bird that wandereth from her nest, so is a man that wandereth from his place.

9 Ointment and perfume rejoice the heart: so doth the sweetness of a man's friend by hearty counsel.

10 Thine own friend, and thy father's friend, forsake not; neither go into thy brother's house in the day of thy calamity: for better is a neighbour that is near than a brother far off.

11 My son, be wise, and make my heart glad, that I may answer him that reproacheth me.

12 A prudent man foreseeth the evil, and hideth himself; but the simple pass on, and are punished.

13 Take his garment that is surety for a stranger, and take a pledge of him for a strange woman.

14 He that blesseth his friend with a loud voice, rising early in the morning, it shall be counted a curse to him.

15 A continual dropping in a very rainy day and a contentious woman are alike.

16 Whosoever hideth her hideth the wind, and the ointment of his right hand, which bewrayeth itself.

17 Iron sharpeneth iron; so a man sharpeneth the countenance of his friend.

18 Whoso keepeth the fig tree shall eat the fruit thereof: so he that waiteth on his master shall be honoured.

19 As in water face answereth to face, so the heart of man to man.

20 Hell and destruction are never full; so the eyes of man are never satisfied.

21 As the fining pot for silver, and the furnace for gold; so is a man to his praise.

22 Though thou shouldest bray a fool in a mortar among wheat with a pestle, yet will not his foolishness depart from him.

23 Be thou diligent to know the state of thy flocks, and look well to thy herds.

24 For riches are not for ever: and doth the crown endure to every generation?

25 The hay appeareth, and the tender grass sheweth itself, and herbs of the mountains are gathered.

26 The lambs are for thy clothing, and the goats are the price of the field.

27 And thou shalt have goats' milk enough for thy food, for the food of thy household, and for the maintenance for thy maidens.

Proverbs Chapter 28

The wicked flee when no man pursueth: but the righteous are bold as a lion.

2 For the transgression of a land many are the princes thereof: but by a man of understanding and knowledge the state thereof shall be prolonged.

3 A poor man that oppresseth the poor is like a sweeping rain which leaveth no food.

4 They that forsake the law praise the wicked: but such as keep the law contend with them.

5 Evil men understand not judgment: but they that seek the Lord understand all things.

6 Better is the poor that walketh in his uprightness, than he that is perverse in his ways, though he be rich.

7 Whoso keepeth the law is a wise son: but he that is a companion of riotous men shameth his father.

8 He that by usury and unjust gain increaseth his substance, he shall gather it for him that will pity the poor.

9 He that turneth away his ear from hearing the law, even his prayer shall be abomination.

10 Whoso causeth the righteous to go astray in an evil way, he shall fall himself into his own pit: but the upright shall have good things in possession.

11 The rich man is wise in his own conceit; but the poor that hath understanding searcheth him out.

12 When righteous men do rejoice, there is great glory: but when the wicked rise, a man is hidden.

13 He that covereth his sins shall not prosper: but whoso confesseth and forsaketh them shall have mercy.

14 Happy is the man that feareth alway: but he that hardeneth his heart shall fall into mischief.

15 As a roaring lion, and a ranging bear; so is a wicked ruler over the poor people.

16 The prince that wanteth understanding is also a great oppressor: but he that hateth covetousness shall prolong his days.

17 A man that doeth violence to the blood of any person shall flee to the pit; let no man stay him.

18 Whoso walketh uprightly shall be saved: but he that is perverse in his ways shall fall at once.

19 He that tilleth his land shall have plenty of bread: but he that followeth after vain persons shall have poverty enough.

20 A faithful man shall abound with blessings: but he that maketh haste to be rich shall not be innocent.

21 To have respect of persons is not good: for for a piece of bread that man will transgress.

22 He that hasteth to be rich hath an evil eye, and considereth not that poverty shall come upon him.

23 He that rebuketh a man afterwards shall find more favour than he that flattereth with the tongue.

24 Whoso robbeth his father or his mother, and saith, It is no transgression; the same is the companion of a destroyer.

25 He that is of a proud heart stirreth up strife: but he that putteth his trust in the Lord shall be made fat.

26 He that trusteth in his own heart is a fool: but whoso walketh wisely, he shall be delivered.

27 He that giveth unto the poor shall not lack: but he that hideth his eyes shall have many a curse.

28 When the wicked rise, men hide themselves: but when they perish, the righteous increase..

Proverbs Chapter 29

He, that being often reproved hardeneth his neck, shall suddenly be destroyed, and that without remedy.

2 When the righteous are in authority, the people rejoice: but when the wicked beareth rule, the people mourn.

3 Whoso loveth wisdom rejoiceth his father: but he that keepeth company with harlots spendeth his substance.

4 The king by judgment establisheth the land: but he that receiveth gifts overthroweth it.

5 A man that flattereth his neighbour spreadeth a net for his feet.

6 In the transgression of an evil man there is a snare: but the righteous doth sing and rejoice.

7 The righteous considereth the cause of the poor: but the wicked regardeth not to know it.

8 Scornful men bring a city into a snare: but wise men turn away wrath.

9 If a wise man contendeth with a foolish man, whether he rage or laugh, there is no rest.

10 The bloodthirsty hate the upright: but the just seek his soul.

11 A fool uttereth all his mind: but a wise man keepeth it in till afterwards.

12 If a ruler hearken to lies, all his servants are wicked.

13 The poor and the deceitful man meet together: the Lord lighteneth both their eyes.

14 The king that faithfully judgeth the poor, his throne shall be established for ever.

15 The rod and reproof give wisdom: but a child left to himself bringeth his mother to shame.

16 When the wicked are multiplied, transgression increaseth: but the righteous shall see their fall.

17 Correct thy son, and he shall give thee rest; yea, he shall give delight unto thy soul.

18 Where there is no vision, the people perish: but he that keepeth the law, happy is he.

19 A servant will not be corrected by words: for though he understand he will not answer.

20 Seest thou a man that is hasty in his words? there is more hope of a fool than of him.

21 He that delicately bringeth up his servant from a child shall have him become his son at the length.

22 An angry man stirreth up strife, and a furious man aboundeth in transgression.

23 A man's pride shall bring him low: but honour shall uphold the humble in spirit.

24 Whoso is partner with a thief hateth his own soul: he heareth cursing, and bewrayeth it not.

25 The fear of man bringeth a snare: but whoso putteth his trust in the Lord shall be safe.

26 Many seek the ruler's favour; but every man's judgment cometh from the Lord.

27 An unjust man is an abomination to the just: and he that is upright in the way is abomination to the wicked.

Proverbs Chapter 30

The words of Agur the son of Jakeh, even the prophecy: the man spake unto Ithiel, even unto Ithiel and Ucal,

2 Surely I am more brutish than any man, and have not the understanding of a man.

3 I neither learned wisdom, nor have the knowledge of the holy.

4 Who hath ascended up into heaven, or descended? who hath gathered the wind in his fists? who hath bound the waters in a garment? who hath established all the ends of the earth? what is his name, and what is his son's name, if thou canst tell?

5 Every word of God is pure: he is a shield unto them that put their trust in him.

6 Add thou not unto his words, lest he reprove thee, and thou be found a liar.

7 Two things have I required of thee; deny me them not before I die:

8 Remove far from me vanity and lies: give me neither poverty nor riches; feed me with food convenient for me:

9 Lest I be full, and deny thee, and say, Who is the Lord? or lest I be poor, and steal, and take the name of my God in vain.

10 Accuse not a servant unto his master, lest he curse thee, and thou be found guilty.

11 There is a generation that curseth their father, and doth not bless their mother.

12 There is a generation that are pure in their own eyes, and yet is not washed from their filthiness.

13 There is a generation, O how lofty are their eyes! and their eyelids are lifted up.

14 There is a generation, whose teeth are as swords, and their jaw teeth as knives, to devour the poor from off the earth, and the needy from among men.

15 The horseleach hath two daughters, crying, Give, give. There are three things that are never satisfied, yea, four things say not, It is enough:

16 The grave; and the barren womb; the earth that is not filled with water; and the fire that saith not, It is enough.

17 The eye that mocketh at his father, and despiseth to obey his mother, the ravens of the valley shall pick it out, and the young eagles shall eat it.

18 There be three things which are too wonderful for me, yea, four which I know not:

19 The way of an eagle in the air; the way of a serpent upon a rock; the way of a ship in the midst of the sea; and the way of a man with a maid.

20 Such is the way of an adulterous woman; she eateth, and wipeth her mouth, and saith, I have done no wickedness.

21 For three things the earth is disquieted, and for four which it cannot bear:

22 For a servant when he reigneth; and a fool when he is filled with meat;

23 For an odious woman when she is married; and an handmaid that is heir to her mistress.

24 There be four things which are little upon the earth, but they are exceeding wise:

25 The ants are a people not strong, yet they prepare their meat in the summer;

26 The conies are but a feeble folk, yet make they their houses in the rocks;

27 The locusts have no king, yet go they forth all of them by bands;

28 The spider taketh hold with her hands, and is in kings' palaces.

29 There be three things which go well, yea, four are comely in going:

30 A lion which is strongest among beasts, and turneth not away for any;

31 A greyhound; an he goat also; and a king, against whom there is no rising up.

32 If thou hast done foolishly in lifting up thyself, or if thou hast thought evil, lay thine hand upon thy mouth.

33 Surely the churning of milk bringeth forth butter, and the wringing of the nose bringeth forth blood: so the forcing of wrath bringeth forth strife.

Proverbs Chapter 31

The words of king Lemuel, the prophecy that his mother taught him.

2 What, my son? and what, the son of my womb? and what, the son of my vows?

3 Give not thy strength unto women, nor thy ways to that which destroyeth kings.

4 It is not for kings, O Lemuel, it is not for kings to drink wine; nor for princes strong drink:

5 Lest they drink, and forget the law, and pervert the judgment of any of the afflicted.

6 Give strong drink unto him that is ready to perish, and wine unto those that be of heavy hearts.

7 Let him drink, and forget his poverty, and remember his misery no more.

8 Open thy mouth for the dumb in the cause of all such as are appointed to destruction.

9 Open thy mouth, judge righteously, and plead the cause of the poor and needy.

10 Who can find a virtuous woman? for her price is far above rubies.

11 The heart of her husband doth safely trust in her, so that he shall have no need of spoil.

12 She will do him good and not evil all the days of her life.

13 She seeketh wool, and flax, and worketh willingly with her hands.

14 She is like the merchants' ships; she bringeth her food from afar.

15 She riseth also while it is yet night, and giveth meat to her household, and a portion to her maidens.

16 She considereth a field, and buyeth it: with the fruit of her hands she planteth a vineyard.

17 She girdeth her loins with strength, and strengtheneth her arms.

18 She perceiveth that her merchandise is good: her candle goeth not out by night.

19 She layeth her hands to the spindle, and her hands hold the distaff.

20 She stretcheth out her hand to the poor; yea, she reacheth forth her hands to the needy.

21 She is not afraid of the snow for her household: for all her household are clothed with scarlet.

22 She maketh herself coverings of tapestry; her clothing is silk and purple.

23 Her husband is known in the gates, when he sitteth among the elders of the land.

24 She maketh fine linen, and selleth it; and delivereth girdles unto the merchant.

25 Strength and honour are her clothing; and she shall rejoice in time to come.

26 She openeth her mouth with wisdom; and in her tongue is the law of kindness.

27 She looketh well to the ways of her household, and eateth not the bread of idleness.

28 Her children arise up, and call her blessed; her husband also, and he praiseth her.

29 Many daughters have done virtuously, but thou excellest them all.

30 Favour is deceitful, and beauty is vain: but a woman that feareth the Lord, she shall be praised.

31 Give her of the fruit of her hands; and let her own works praise her in the gates.

Daily Prayer of Protection

LORD please remove my flesh far away from your will for
my life, so I won't have to pay later for a bad decision my
flesh could and would make today. Thank You JESUS!
AMEN

When we hear a word from GOD, it informs us. When we receive
and believe the word from GOD, it transforms us. Hallelujah!

WHAT?
DO YOU EXPECT FROM A SINNER
BY CLAUDIA RENÉE

www.ingramcontent.com/pod-product-compliance
Lightning Source LLC
Chambersburg PA
CBHW051447250726
48655CB00001B/288